What People are Saying About
EFT AND THE GETTING THRU TECHNIQUES

"This is the medicine of the future."

- Rudolph Ballentine, M.D.
Author of *Radical Healing*

"As a long-time healer, I found *Getting Thru to Your Emotions with EFT* [Emotional Freedom Techniques] to greatly enhance my own healing skills. Anyone who wants to find wholeness for themselves and others will be richly rewarded by the detailed guidance found in this book."
- Walter Weston
Author of *Healing Yourself*

"In my estimation, EFT is one of the most powerful treatments available. I have successfully treated fears, phobias, depression, and addictions. It is rapid, dramatic, and deep." - Fred Gallo, PhD
Author of *Energy Psychology*

"This book is a veritable gold mine of information. I keep it handy as a 'must have' database of information." - Wayne Clayton Robb
Clinical Hypnotherapist/Cognitive Therapist

"The GTT techniques have helped me to speak my own truth without fear of what others think and expect of me." - Steve Chroniak
Book Store Events Coordinator, Yoga and Meditation Teacher

"After taking Jane's EFT class, I achieved a decreased anxiety level with this simple technique that was profound. I discovered a peace I'd never experienced before." - Cathy Paris
Sales Representative

"I have had a fear of flying for about twenty years. One time the fear was so intense I got off the plane right before the stewardess shut the door. When I took Phillip and Jane's EFT Class, they helped me to prepare for a trip the following month. I again started doing the techniques about a week before my flight. I tapped before the trip and several times when I felt the need during the flight. Returning home, I didn't need to tap at all, but did it before the flight just for the heck of it. I was actually very relaxed. I put all my faith in this, but still I was so surprised when it worked. What a relief!" - Irene Licini
Homemaker

"By using GTT [Getting Thru Techniques], I was able to get past my anger and forgive all those involved and get on with my life path. If it hadn't been for these processes, I probably would have been bitter and resentful for many years." - Terry Burke
Pharmacist, Hypnotherapist, Reiki Master

"EFT helps me check in with myself, particularly when I've lost my center. For my massage clients, it helps remove emotional problems so the body can heal faster." - Kathi Gibson
Massage Therapist, Hypnotherapist

"I overcame my panic of test-taking and public speaking with EFT. I am amazingly calm after doing it. I don't think I've ever taken a test in such a calm state." - Sharon Shiflett
Teacher

"Phillip and Jane Mountrose give the step-by-step information to clear and eliminate a wide array of common problems. *Getting Thru to Your Emotions with EFT* offers the next generation in healing. A great resource!"
                                            - Katherine Zimmerman
                                            author of *Breakthrough: EFT*

"EFT is an extraordinary healing process. My wife has found freedom from her agrophobia [fear of going places] that she has not experienced in over 40 years since it began."
                                            - Patrick Raab
                                            Massage Therapist

"In my quest for spiritual growth and emotional health, I have learned just about every healing modality. EFT is one of the most amazing. In a few minutes you can release stress, emotions, and habits it took a lifetime to acquire."
                                            - Helaine Ellis
                                            Hypnotherapist, Healer

"I helped a friend remove pain in his arm by using EFT. It has also cleared blockages for my spiritual growth. I find it works really well."
                                            - Richard Fry
                                            Pharmacist, Reiki Master

"It's unbelievable how quickly a shift can occur with EFT. I recently experienced the death of my sister. As it happened, I received the call at Jane's EFT class, just moments before it started. I couldn't keep from crying, but felt that it would be best to stay. When the class began, Jane had me do one of the EFT techniques. It helped me to immediately detach from the sadness and inner pain and allowed me to continue on in the class that evening. The sadness returns every once in awhile, but, with EFT, I'm able to accept the loss in a realistic way."
                                            - Marion Hakata
                                            Hypnotherapist, Reiki Master, and Teacher

Book and Cover Design
By Jane Mountrose

GETTING THRU TO YOUR EMOTIONS WITH EFT

Phillip Mountrose and Jane Mountrose

Holistic Communications
Sacramento, California

Published by: Holistic Communications
                 P.O. Box 41152
                 Sacramento, CA 95841-0152 USA
                 E-mail: eft@gettingthru.org

ISBN: 0-9653787-6-4
Library of Congress Catalog Card Number: 99-095415

Publisher's Cataloging-in-Publication
    (*Provided by Quality Books Inc.*)

Mountrose, Phillip.
Getting thru to your emotions with EFT : tap into your hidden
potential with the emotional freedom techniques / Phillip Mountrose
and Jane Mountrose – 1st ed.
p. cm
Includes biographical references and index.
LCCN: 99-95415
ISBN 0-9653787-6-4
1. Self-actualization (Psychology). 2. Mind and body. 3. Emotions.
I. Mountrose, Jane. II. Title.

BF637.S4M68 2000   158.1
                     QBI99-1206

Acknowledgments

This book is about achieving genuine emotional freedom. We have been fortunate to meet many wonderful and talented people who have contributed to our understanding. They have helped us in innumerable ways as we have moved forward on our own journeys of self-discovery, and in the development of the techniques we use in our work helping others.

A book on EFT would not be complete without thanking Gary Craig and Adrienne Fowlie for developing the Emotional Freedom Techniques and making them so readily available to others. Through his Web site (www.emofree.com) and e-mail forum, Gary Craig continues to provide updates on the use of these techniques. His genuine desire to help to educate others in what is possible is inspiring.

We also want to thank Barry Snyder and Karen Anderson for leading us on the path that has produced the Getting Thru Techniques.

In addition, we thank Briana Finley for her insightful input in the writing of this book. Also, we would like to add our appreciation to all of the people who, through classes and personal consultations, have provided examples for this book, and helped us to refine our use of the techniques. They have provided encouragement and invaluable support.

Publisher's Disclaimer

The Emotional Freedom Techniques (EFT) and the Getting Thru Techniques (GTT) have helped many people to make positive changes in their lives, but there is no guarantee they will work for you. We do not recommend substituting these techniques for the professional services of a doctor, psychologist or psychiatrist. Please consult your medical health professionals regarding their use.

EFT and GTT are self-help and self-healing techniques and you are in control of their use. As such, you have sole responsibility when you use them. If you do not wish to be bound by this disclaimer, you may return this book with proof of purchase to the publisher for a full refund.

Table of Contents

Table of Figures

Foreword

By opening this book, you have entered the doorway to the new Healing High-Rise.

This doorway leads to new discoveries in the field of human potential that are creating miraculous changes in people's lives that only a few years ago were deemed impossible. As you open the door and step inside, your possibilities for healing will vastly increase. This book provides a powerful array of techniques that just about anyone can use to overcome obstacles to experiencing genuine emotional freedom.

In 1991, I had the opportunity to study a meridian-based healing system under the tutelage of Dr. Roger Callahan. By 1995, I transformed and simplified those remarkable procedures into a form that just about anyone can use. I call it Emotional Freedom Techniques (EFT for short). Phillip and Jane Mountrose have done a superb job in bringing you the essence of these discoveries... and more.

Some are understandably skeptical of the validity of these processes. Such doubts always accompany new breakthroughs and innovations. But the proof is in the dramatic results, and, not surprisingly, many therapists are drawn to the speed and effectiveness of EFT.

EFT is simple, relatively painless, quick and can be self-administered. Further, it can provide relief for an extraordinary range of problems. After years of developing these techniques, my jaw still drops at the many "one minute wonders" people experience, sometimes eliminating what were severe problems that had been around for decades. But even when the cases are more complex, it often takes only a few sessions for the client to gain relief. It is rare for a problem to take weeks or months with EFT.

EFT and the Getting Thru Techniques address the whole energy system. They help you to transcend old paradigms and stubborn problems. The processes are designed to bring you to wholeness, often in more dramatic and effective ways than you might imagine possible.

So explore this new Healing High-Rise with Phillip and Jane. Let this dedicated pair help you fulfill your potential, clear blockages, and move upward within the Healing High-Rise. The view from the top is spectacular!

Gary Craig
The Sea Ranch, California
August 1999

Part 1

GETTING STARTED AT GETTING THRU

CHAPTER ONE

Welcome to the Healing High-Rise

The real voyage of discovery consists not in seeking new lands but seeing with new eyes.

- MARCEL PROUST

Would you like to know how to be more successful at whatever you choose to do? What about knowing how to lose weight without starving and being able to maintain it for life? Would you like to know how you can reduce pain and improve your overall health and well-being? This is just a glimpse of what the information in this book can help you to do.

You are about to explore some emotional clearing techniques that many consider a modern miracle. They are based on a series of discoveries that some psychologists consider to be among the most important breakthroughs in their field in the twentieth century. EFT, the Emotional Freedom Techniques, is a group of techniques that just about anyone can learn to use to release the stuck emotions that prevent them from experiencing happiness and moving forward toward their goals in life. These techniques were developed and introduced in 1995 by Gary Craig and Adrienne Fowlie, based on the work of psychologist Dr. Roger Callahan.

In its short history, EFT has already helped thousands of people with a vast array of common emotions, including:

- Stress and anxiety.

- Anger and frustration.

- Depression.

- All kinds of fears and phobias.

- Negative memories and inner child issues.

- Self-doubt.

- Guilt, grief, confusion and just about any other emotion imaginable, including those icky, yucky and generally awful feelings you can't even find a name for.

Amazingly, the benefits do not end there. EFT is not limited to releasing painful emotions. Consider these possibilities:

1. **Improve your health:**

   - Reduce physical cravings for substances like chocolate and cigarettes.

   - Relieve pain.

   - Overcome insomnia.

   - Increase your overall well-being.

2. Increase your effectiveness in everything you do:

- Expand your career opportunities.

- Improve your performance in sports, your career, and any aspect of your life.

- Release your limitations about money and open to creating more abundance in your life.

- Improve your business and personal relationships.

- Speak up in public situations and with those you are not able to communicate with now.

3. Improve the quality of your life:

- Release any feelings that prevent you from experiencing a life filled with joy and love.

- Build up the courage to try the things you have always wanted to do, but never dared.

- Enhance your personal and spiritual growth process.

There are almost countless of examples of people who have recovered with ease from emotions that have disturbed them for years using EFT. It has been shown to be effective where other techniques have failed. It has even been used successfully for relieving a variety of physical symptoms like headaches and back pain, along with conditions such as insomnia. EFT is particularly helpful when the physical symptoms are directly linked to emotions like stress and anxiety. The success rate reported by the developers of EFT when dealing with emotions is between 80 percent and 100 percent. This has been our experience as well. With physical conditions, the success rate is lower, but many people suffering from a wide variety of conditions have received tremendous benefits from the use of EFT. In many cases, the effects are permanent and, if not, the procedure may be easily repeated.

EFT is also gentle and works quickly. Most EFT users are able to release troubling emotions like fear, anxiety, anger, and stress in a short time, often within a single session or several days or weeks compared with months or years of traditional therapy. These types of techniques are so effective that their originator, Dr. Callahan, reportedly went bankrupt when he began using his techniques with his clients, because they recovered so quickly.

One of the things we appreciate most is EFT's versatility. When you have mastered these skills, it is almost like having superpowers. You will have tools that you can use in just about any situation. For instance, if you are going into an important meeting or interview and feel anxious or afraid, you can just sit in your car or duck quickly into the restroom and do some EFT. It works wonders and doesn't require any special equipment, so you can use it virtually anywhere.

THE GETTING THRU TECHNIQUES

"Getting Thru to Your Emotions" is about connecting in a profound way with the truth of who you are. In addition to EFT, this book includes techniques drawn from our extensive experience with Hypnotherapy, NLP, Kinesiology, Reiki and other holistic healing modalities. Refer to the Glossary for more information about these approaches. The unique techniques we have developed form the heart of the Getting Thru Approach. They enhance any healing process and help you to bring more awareness to whatever you are going through.

Through our experience, we have come to regard life as a

journey of self-discovery and find that there are always deeper levels of ourselves to explore. Each of us is here with lessons to learn and a purpose to fulfill. As we step forward on our journeys, we face challenges that help us to learn these lessons and grow as individuals. This in turn helps us to expand our awareness collectively as a society.

From a spiritual perspective, our problems are opportunities to increase our understanding of the deeper meaning of life and our true purpose.

The combination of EFT and the Getting Thru Techniques can help you to move rapidly along on this journey by releasing your fears, unresolved emotions and all types of limitations, so you can experience a life filled with joy, love and freedom to fulfill your heart's true desires. To simplify, we will refer to the Getting Thru Techniques as GTT.

When we began our own exploration of personal and spiritual growth in the 1970's, there was nothing like EFT or GTT. Like most people, we thought that true growth and enlightenment were extremely difficult to achieve and only possible for people like monks and mystics in far-off caves or monasteries.

Times change, as does human potential. One of the greatest challenges with EFT is opening the mind enough to consider that it is possible to overcome stubborn emotional patterns in a short time. People often come to us believing that their emotional patterns are going to be difficult and painful to release. The limiting beliefs are often more challenging than the emotions themselves.

Craig and Fowlie report having similar experiences in their *Emotional Freedom Techniques Manual,* where they state:

You hold in your hand a major innovation. As you will see, it is based on the soundest of scientific principles. But because it is so dramatically different from "conventional wisdom," it is consistently and understandably greeted with skepticism. EFT is not alone in this. Other innovations have met with similar attitudes.

They go on to list a number of examples of these limiting beliefs, such as "Everything that can be invented has been invented," a quote from Charles H. Duell, the Director of the U.S. Patent Office, from 1899. That obviously was not true at the end of the 19th century and certainly is not true as we venture into the 21st century. By keeping an open mind to these techniques, you can allow the results to speak for themselves.

With techniques like EFT and GTT, we are on the ground floor of what Craig calls a "healing high-rise." We also see ourselves on the edge of a new era, an age of self-realization. We are at the point in the evolution of humanity when every individual has the opportunity to attain wholeness and achieve the love, joy, and freedom that we all deeply long for. With this in mind, it is no surprise that approaches like EFT and GTT are beginning to emerge, creating almost unlimited possibilities for anyone who wants to expand and grow.

EXPLORING THE TECHNIQUES

This book can take you on an adventure of self-discovery. It is like a treasure chest filled with priceless tools that you can explore and adapt to meet your needs. It includes general information about EFT and GTT, step-by-step instructions on each of the techniques, and examples from our experience. You will also learn how these techniques can contribute to your personal growth, leading to balance and wholeness in your life.

As with anything new, the key to success with these techniques is practice. All of the EFT techniques are easy to do, but there are some subtleties that can affect your results. The GTT processes go deeper and may take more time to master, particularly for those who are new to self-exploration. We suggest reading over the whole book while you start practicing the first one or two techniques. Practice each technique in the order presented until you feel comfortable enough to move on to the next. This will allow you to develop competence and eliminate some troubling emotions along the way.

Like other healing modalities, you may find EFT and GTT to be more effective when done with another person. We recommend sharing this experience with a person or group of people who are open-minded, supportive, and ready to move forward in their lives.

When a group of people with a common goal of healing come together in an environment of love and acceptance, the results are magnified many times.

You can also help each other to learn more about yourselves by bringing in a variety of perspectives.

We all know the phrase: "You can lead a horse to water, but you can't make it drink." This book points the way, but the effort is up to you. With all of the self-help books available today, there is a tendency to learn a little about a lot of things, without becoming skilled at any. It may be easier to move on to the next book than to take the time to become proficient with the techniques you find here. But we hope you will stop and take a good look at what you have found first.

This book can transform your life. It is the result of twenty-five years of dedication and trial and error, which has resulted in the development and incorporation of some of the most powerful tools available today. If you devote as little as fifteen minutes a day to these techniques, your life will improve in unimaginable ways.

RECORDING YOUR EXPERIENCES

We recommend keeping a written journal of your experiences with EFT and GTT. You should notice some wonderful changes in your life if you continue to use these techniques, and keeping a journal allows you to bring awareness to these changes. Writing helps you to maintain your focus and integrate your experiences.

So why do so many people avoid writing things down? When you put something down on paper, you can't ignore it. It becomes concrete. This is also its value. In fact, studies show that people who write down their goals are much more likely to achieve them. Writing down your experiences helps you to integrate them and reach new levels of understanding. It also reinforces your commitment to your development. Refer to Figure 1.1 for a summary of the reasons for keeping a journal.

TAKING CONTROL OF YOUR LIFE

Before starting to use the techniques in this book, we want to let you know that you are in control. Like coaches, we are available to teach you some effective methods for helping yourself. You are free to progress in your own way and at your own pace. We are not licensed psychologists or medical health professionals. We are ordained Ministers of Holistic Healing and serve others as spiritual counselors and teachers.

The purpose of this book is to help you to deal with the

FIGURE 1.1
KEEPING A WRITTEN JOURNAL

Keeping a written journal is a key to success in making powerful changes in your life. It will help you to:

- **Stay Focused:** You can use your journal to write down your goals, record your successes, and make a note of things you want to remember later.

- **Record New Levels of Awareness:** You will probably understand your life in a new way as you progress with the techniques in this book. It is easier to recall these new understandings and access them in the future if you write them down.

- **Validate Your Multi-Dimensional Reality:** With EFT and GTT, you will have an opportunity to explore parts of yourself that you may not even know exist. You will want to have a record of what you discover.

- **Access Unconscious Feelings:** The act of writing in itself can help you to access information from deeper levels of your awareness as the words flow out on the paper.

- **Integrate Your Experiences:** Writing your experiences and understandings can help you to ingrain the experience more deeply in your conscious awareness.

---

kinds of challenges that normal people face in the course of their lives, and to help you to heal them holistically. We do not recommend substituting these techniques for the professional services of doctors, psychologists, and psychiatrists. We recommend having their permission before using any of these techniques.

Fortunately, these techniques are practically risk-free. Gary Craig reported in his *EFT Training Manual* that after using the techniques for six years on behalf of hundreds of people, he observed no material side effects. EFT does not involve the use of needles, chemicals, or invasive surgical procedures. EFT includes gentle tapping in specific places on the body, humming, counting, and rotating your eyes. Dr. Callahan, whose TFT (Thought Field Therapy) processes are similar, has performed his techniques on thousands of people. He reported no side effects except the rare occasion when people bruised themselves from tapping too hard. This, of course, is unnecessary.

Although experts in the field have observed no significant side effects, a few people have had reactions. Craig and Fowlie mention these examples in their *EFT Training Manual.*

- Craig reported that several ladies told him that they felt mildly nauseated after doing the tapping. In all cases, the nausea went away after a short time.

- Craig reported using EFT in a restaurant with a woman who had been abused sexually as a child. As he began to guide her in the use of EFT, her memories of the abuse became increasingly intense. Since they were in a public place, he became concerned and decided to stop working with her. No problem occurred after that.

- A friend of Craig's, working with a large group of people with fibromyalgia, reported that a few of them became weak in the knees while doing EFT and had to sit down. Gary has not had this experience himself.

- A professional therapist called in Craig to help a very disturbed lady with EFT. The EFT tapping techniques relaxed her to such a degree that she fell into a deep sleep. The therapist woke her up an hour later, but apparently the woman was still sleepy on the way home and got into an auto accident. Craig suggested that common sense is needed in such cases.

Craig and Fowlie also took a survey of 250 therapists, asking them to respond with any serious reactions by their clients using EFT and Dr. Callahan's TFT techniques. Out of 10,000 uses, they reported 20 incidences. Most of the reactions were reported by seriously disturbed patients.

The purpose of citing these examples is to let you know that it is highly unlikely that you will experience a negative reaction from these techniques. Nonetheless, as Gary Craig says,

That does not mean you won't have a problem. You or someone you help with EFT may be an exception. As I'm sure you can appreciate, Adrienne and I will not assume responsibility in this regard. The responsibility for your emotional and physical well-being must rest with you.

We likewise hand the responsibility for the use of the EFT and GTT techniques in this book over to you.

We conclude with the following statements, which also come directly from Craig and Fowlie. We pass them on as our agreement with you, our readers. We also include in this agreement the use of the GTT techniques along with EFT.

- You are required to take complete responsibility for your own emotional and/or physical well-being....

- You are also required to instruct others whom you help with EFT (and GTT) to take complete responsibility for their emotional and /or physical well-being.

- You must agree to hold harmless Gary Craig, Adrienne Fowlie, and anyone involved with EFT from any claims made by anyone whom you seek to help with EFT (and GTT).

- We urge you to use these techniques under the supervision of a qualified psychologist or physician. Don't use these techniques to try to solve a problem where your common sense would tell you it is not appropriate.

If you are not able to agree with these statements, please do not read further and do not use the techniques in his book.

CHAPTER TWO

Prepare for Healing on All Levels

*Your future depends on many things,
but mostly on you.*

- FRANK TYGER

EFT is one of a number of meridian-based techniques that are now being developed worldwide. It works by tapping on a series of points on the body that correspond to acupuncture points in the energy meridian system. For those who are unfamiliar with the meridian system and the acupuncture points, we will describe them later in this chapter.

Dr. Callahan, the psychotherapist who taught Craig and Fowlie the transformational power of tapping on acupuncture points to clear emotional patterns, has used his techniques in the development of a series of processes that he now calls TFT (Thought Field Therapy).

Dr. Callahan came upon his first discovery by chance while

working with a woman who had been troubled by a fear of water for many years. After working with her for about a year and a half without much success, she mentioned in a session that along with the fear, she was experiencing discomfort in her stomach. Having studied the energy meridians, Dr. Callahan knew that the stomach meridian starts just below the eye. Out of curiosity and with her permission, he tapped a few times on this point below her eye with his fingertips. To their amazement, her water phobia disappeared instantaneously.

This was around 1980 and, to our knowledge, her fear of water never returned. Dr. Callahan admitted that this first case was beginner's luck. Most emotional patterns do not clear by tapping on just one point, but he had made an important discovery. From this experience, he developed tapping sequences for a variety of different emotional conditions. Those who have followed the extraordinary success of his work credit him with one of the greatest discoveries in this field in the twentieth century.

As previously mentioned, two such people are Gary Craig and Adrienne Fowlie, who developed the Emotional Freedom Techniques (EFT). Gary's background is in engineering, rather than psychology. As a pragmatist, he has geared EFT toward use by virtually anyone who wants to make improvements in his or her life.

While TFT uses different tapping sequences for specific emotional patterns, EFT provides two generalized sequences that may be used for any emotional disturbance. Craig compares it to doing a car repair. TFT identifies exactly where the problem is and deals with it directly, like doing an analysis of a car's condition and repairing each of the parts that are not working. This, of course, requires a high degree of skill and expertise. EFT uses generalized sequences and repairs all of the parts each time, dealing with the problem universally. This is why EFT is so easy to use. No special skill or understanding of the meridian system is required for these processes to work.

A HOLISTIC APPROACH TO EFT

In this book, we add the techniques we have learned and developed in our teaching and spiritual counseling work. As previously mentioned, we both have extensive experience with Hypnotherapy, NLP, Reiki, Kinesiology, and now EFT. Phillip also has over twenty years of experience in education, including working with emotionally disturbed teenage boys. He has shared some of this experience in his two books *Getting Thru to Kids: Problem Solving with Children Ages 6 to 18* and *Tips and Tools for Getting Thru to Kids.*

As we explored these different modalities and worked with students and clients in person and over the telephone, we gradually developed our abilities to perceive energy and the power of holistic healing in a variety of ways. We learned to feel energy with our hands and to see it with our inner vision. We can detect where energetic blockages exist in and around the body, and perceive energetic changes occurring as they are released. We can also help others to reach into the recesses of the mind and release blockages at that level.

True healing is holistic. It considers all of the parts of the whole and deals with the source of the problem, rather than relieving the symptoms.

As we continue to open to new forms of healing, we have become more and more aware of how everything is connected.

Any emotional disturbance also has a mental, spiritual, and sometimes even a physical component. True healing includes clearing the blockages on all four levels and expands our understanding of ourselves.

To validate our perceptions of how the mind, emotions and body are all connected, we can refer to recent scientific research. Since the early 1970's, the field of brain research has been revolutionized by the discovery of neurotransmitters, minute chemicals that transmit impulses between the brain and the cells of the body. Dr. Deepak Chopra, MD, an endocrinologist who is at the forefront of mindbody medicine, describes this process in his book *Quantum Healing*:

> Neurotransmitters are the runners that race to and from the brain, telling every organ inside us of our emotions, desires, memories, intuitions, and dreams. None of these events are confined to the brain alone. Likewise, none of them are strictly mental, since they can be coded into chemical messages. Neurotransmitters touch the life of every cell. Wherever a thought wants to go, these chemicals must go too, and without them, no thoughts can exist. To think is to practice brain chemistry, promoting a cascade of responses throughout the body.

The discovery of neurotransmitters provides scientific proof that the body, emotions, and mind are all connected. Now members of the medical community all over the country are making profound observations about the connection between the mind and body in their patients. Dr. Chopra also says:

> In my own practice, several cancer patients have recovered completely after being pronounced incurable and given only a few months to live. I didn't think they were miracles; I thought they were proof that the mind can go deep enough to change the very patterns that design the body. It can wipe mistakes off the blue-

print, so to speak, and destroy any disease — cancer, diabetes, coronary heart disease — that has disturbed the design.

What we are beginning to understand is that negative thoughts and emotions can be extremely harmful to our well-being at all levels, physically, emotionally, mentally and even spiritually. No one would intentionally produce thoughts that make them depressed or unhappy, defeat their chances of realizing their dreams and goals, cause weight gain, generate stress in the body, or produce physical illness. Yet, this happens all of the time.

The origin of the negative thoughts and emotions that plague us is the unconscious mind. And, since it has generally been left unobserved, the unconscious mind responds in the best way it can based on input it has received from ourselves, our families, peers, business associates, and society as a whole.

The most powerful resource you can access through the unconscious is the True Self or Soul, which is the spiritual part of your nature.

From a holistic point of view, we are spiritual beings who have a physical body, a mind, and emotions. Through the unconscious mind, we can tap into the Soul, which different people may also refer to as the Creative Intelligence, Spiritual Essence, Inner Guide, or Inner Wisdom.

The Soul knows the answers to all of our questions about the meaning of life, who we really are, and what our true purposes are. This part of us is not fooled by what other people say about us, or by what we say about ourselves. This is why taking a holistic approach is so important. Everything that is happening in our lives physically, emotionally, mentally and spiritually is giving us information about ourselves. When we are able to connect with the Soul, we can find out what we need to learn from our experiences to change for the better.

THE FOUR LEVELS OF HEALING

With EFT and GTT, we are moving into the realm of energetic healing. For many people, this may be a new concept, and one that raises doubts. Fortunately, you do not have to agree with these concepts for the techniques to work. The energetic model also provides a logical sequence for the healing process.

Figure 2.1 illustrates this sequence with "The Four Levels of Healing." These levels form our multi-dimensional reality. They also correspond to the first four layers of the human energy field or aura.

When we are healthy and balanced, we are able to be a full expression of the Soul and are free of energetic interference on all four levels.

Unfortunately, this is not generally the case. Most of us have blockages in our energy fields that create problems at all levels. True healing involves clearing these blockages, so we can experience a state of balance and wholeness.

Energetically, imbalance enters the aura from the outside and travels inward through the spiritual, mental, emotional, and etheric (energetic physical) layers, in that order. At each level we find specific types of patterns. There are separation and judgment at the spiritual level, limiting beliefs and attitudes at the mental level, unresolved emotions at the emotional level, and pain and discomfort at the physical level.

FIGURE 2.1
THE FOUR LEVELS OF HEALING

HEALING JOURNEY GOES	FROM	UNCONSCIOUS EXPRESSION OF THE EGO	TO	CONSCIOUS EXPRESSION OF THE SOUL
Physically	From	Pain, discomfort and illness, where physical vitality is suppressed	To	A sense of physical well-being, comfort and vitality
Emotionally	From	Painful unresolved emotions and a lack of joy	To	Emotional understanding and a joyful experience of life
Mentally	From	Limiting beliefs and attitudes, which create limited possibilities in the world	To	Unlimited thinking and possibilities in the world; genuine freedom
Spiritually	From	Judgment of self and others, feelings of shame and separation	To	A loving existence with feelings of being a part of a unified whole

You could compare the way imbalance steps down through the levels of the aura to stepping down a staircase. At the top of the staircase, which represents balance and harmony, we experience joy, love and freedom. As imbalance enters the aura, we step down into a quagmire of fears, pains, low self-concepts and limitations.

The diagram below shows how imbalance starts at the spiritual level and travels through the layers of the aura, ultimately reaching the emotional and physical levels, where we detect problems in our lives. A holistic approach to healing travels back up, clearing the imbalance in each layer, to return to the experience of joy, love, and freedom.

TOP OF THE STAIRS
Balance and Harmony:
Joy, Love, and Freedom

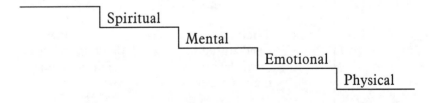

BOTTOM OF THE STAIRS
Imbalance:
Unresolved Emotions, Limiting
Beliefs, and Judgments

Holistic healing systematically clears the physical, emotional, mental and spiritual levels, which we will call PEM&S.

At the top of the stairs, there is also a higher degree of conscious awareness and moving down the stairs, there is a lower degree of conscious awareness. In the quagmire of fears and pains, we are largely unconscious of what is happening to us. So a key to change is awareness. We have to become conscious of what the problem is and how it is affecting us.

To understand how you may be unconscious of what is happening, just look at any part of your life that is disharmonious. It could be a relationship, your job, money, or your sense of fulfillment. You obviously know that something is wrong, but most likely you do not know what is happening within you that is causing the disharmony.

Many people feel trapped financially or unfulfilled in their chosen careers. They probably have no idea what is causing the imbalance. Most hope that the lottery will take care of them sooner or later. Realistically, they have a far better chance of solving their problems by looking within themselves.

With one client, whom we will call Kerry, Jane could see that there was a barrier between her and achieving fulfillment in life. Kerry had no idea what the problem was, but she knew that she was capable of more. By exploring her feelings with GTT, Kerry recognized that from the time she was a small child, she felt that she had to be invisible, so people would not notice her. This made her feel trapped, which caused anger. She also felt sad about the time she had lost when she could have been accomplishing more.

Once Jane and Kerry understood what the problem was, they used EFT. Kerry was able to quickly release the emotions that were holding the experience of being unfulfilled in place, so she could move forward with confidence. With increased awareness and EFT, the barrier was easily removed.

THE MERIDIAN SYSTEM

In our energetic model, the meridian system is the interface between the energy field and the physical body. Where there are blockages in the energy field, there are corresponding disruptions in flow of energy through the meridian system. These blockages are, in turn, reflected in the unconscious patterns (thoughts and emotions) in the mind and in the functioning of the physical body.

ENERGETIC BLOCKAGES IN LAYERS OF THE AURA	=	DISRUPTIONS IN THE MERIDIAN SYSTEM	=	UNCONSCIOUS THOUGHTS AND FEELINGS IN THE MIND

As noted, being effective with EFT does not require an understanding of the meridian system. We are just providing an overview, so you will have a general idea of what is happening when you use EFT. The meridians are channels that transmit energy upward and downward through the body. Each one is associated with an organ system in the body, so they have names like the stomach meridian and the lung meridian. Each one is also associated with specific emotional patterns. For example, the kidney meridian is often associated with fear and the liver meridian is associated with anger.

Together, the meridians form a unified energy system. The end of one meridian is the beginning of the next one, so energy flows continuously through the system. The acupuncture points are all located along these energy channels and through the acupuncture points, you can send energy through the meridian system. There are also side channels that run between meridians, creating more connections.

EFT involves tapping on acupuncture points that are either at the beginning or end of various meridians, sending energy through an entire meridian from each point, and covering the whole system by tapping on a series of points. For EFT to work, you have to perform the tapping while focusing on a specific issue you intend to clear. Focusing on the problem sets up a disruption in the meridian system that is then cleared by the tapping.

Gary Craig describes the basic principle behind his work in this way: "The cause of all emotional problems is a disruption in the body's energy system." It follows, then, that the primary function of EFT is to release the disruptions in the energy system by tapping on specific acupuncture points.

Sometimes we know we have unresolved emotions that need to be cleared to move forward in our lives. At other times, our next steps may be less obvious, but we know that we have not reached the goal yet. When this happens, ask yourself: Where in my life am I not experiencing joy, love and freedom? Your answer will show you what is preventing you from being your personal best. From there, you can begin to examine what is in your way and release it with EFT and GTT.

THE FOUR PARTS OF THIS BOOK

We have divided this book into four parts, which provide a structure for learning the techniques. This structure will also help you to access any information you are looking for easily.

You will also find many examples of processes we have done with our students and clients. We have changed their names to maintain their privacy.

Part 1:
Getting Started At Getting Thru

The purpose of this part of the book is to give you some background on EFT and GTT. No special knowledge is required to achieve success with these techniques. However, having an understanding of the human energy field, the meridian system and the mind explains the nature of holistic healing and demonstrates why these tools are so powerful.

Part 2:
Mastering the Emotional Freedom Techniques

We have mentioned that EFT includes a series of processes. For a newcomer to meridian-based techniques, they may seem unusual, awkward, and even a bit strange at first. Watching a group of people doing EFT is an unusual sight, and may not correspond to our concepts of what doing healing work looks like. In our classes, we often have the whole group tapping at once, and have to admit that we look pretty silly. But, as the saying goes, the proof is in the pudding. The results often seem miraculous and the enthusiasm the group experiences as we see one success after another is extremely rewarding.

Each EFT technique serves a specific purpose. We will provide an overview of them here and explain each one in detail in the chapters that follow.

Part 2 of the book includes:

1. **The Short Sequence:** This is the starting point for using EFT. The Short Sequence only takes about a minute and is effective most of the time. With each use, it clears one aspect of an emotion, so it is often repeated to entirely clear the emotion.

2. **The Floor-to-Ceiling Eye Roll:** This is a short procedure to use when a blockage is almost gone. It will generally remove whatever is left, so you can experience complete relief.

3. **The Complete Sequence:** When you are not getting the desired results with the Short Sequence, you can switch to this longer tapping sequence. After using EFT over a period of years, Gary Craig reports that he hardly ever needs to use the Complete Sequence, because his success is so great with the Short Sequence. This has been our experience as well.

   The Complete Sequence is like a sandwich with another technique, the Nine Gamut Process, wedged between two longer tapping sequences. While the Complete Sequence takes more time than the Short Sequence, it still only takes a few minutes and provides a wonderful tune-up. As with the Short Sequence, each time you use this sequence, it clears one aspect of an emotion, so it may need to be repeated.

4. **The Use of Kinesiology with EFT:** If you are still not receiving the desired results after using the Complete Sequence, you can use Kinesiology, which is muscle testing, to determine the exact nature of an emotional blockage. It can increase your success rate by pinpointing what you have encountered.

5. **The Collarbone Breathing Exercise:** The Collarbone Breathing Exercise is a process developed by Dr. Callahan to overcome a condition known as Neurological Disorganization. It is rarely needed, but it only takes a few minutes to complete, so it is a good option to have available if the other techniques are not producing results.

6. **Dealing with Energy Toxins:** As Dr. Callahan continued to work with the small minority of people who could not be helped by any of his tapping techniques, he discovered that

sometimes toxins in the environment, on the body or within the body can prevent a person from healing. This rarely occurs, but it is helpful to know about it. We also describe how to use Kinesiology to disclose the nature of energy toxins.

Figure 2.2, "When to Use EFT," provides a guide for using each of the Emotional Freedom Techniques.

Part 3:
Going Deeper with the Getting Thru Techniques

Part 3 enlarges on EFT with the Getting Thru Techniques (GTT). These processes bring awareness to what is occurring in the unconscious mind and help the person receiving EFT to understand what is happening holistically as a blockage is cleared. The purpose of these procedures is to reach into the mind to learn more about yourself, to release blockages at a deeper level, and to make powerful changes.

Part 3 includes:

1. **The Holistic Process:** This focusing procedure forms the heart of our Getting Thru Approach and demonstrates the essence of holistic healing. It helps you to uncover what is happening on all levels: physically, emotionally, mentally and spiritually. Once you know what the issues are, you use EFT to clear the blockages. The Holistic Process is a powerful tool for overcoming any type of problem you may encounter.

2. **The Unification Process:** This is a guided visualization process. It takes the Holistic Process a step further by connecting you with the specific part of yourself associated with a problem, and reuniting that part with your Soul. It incorporates the Holistic Process and EFT, so you can clear any blockages you encounter along the way.

FIGURE 2.2
WHEN TO USE EFT

EFT is fast and effective with most emotions. It sometimes produces results with physical conditions as well. Familiarize yourself with these techniques in the order presented before trying the Getting Thru Techniques.

PROCESS	RECOMMENDED USE
The Short Sequence	This is the starting place with EFT.
The Complete Sequence	If you are experiencing little or no relief from your problem with the Short Sequence, try this one next.
The Floor-to-Ceiling Eye Roll	If you have almost completely cleared a problem with the Short and/or Complete Sequences, use this technique to remove the rest.
Kinesiology	If you are having little or no relief with the Short and Complete Sequences, try this next.
The Collarbone Breathing Exercise	If you are having little or no success with the Short and Complete Sequences, or Kinesiology, try this next. You can also try this technique instead of Kinesiology, if you are not comfortable doing muscle testing.
Testing For Energy Toxins	If you are still not having success after trying the Collarbone Breathing Exercise, try this next.

---

3. **The Break Thru Process:** This is another guided visualization, which is designed to use along with the Unification Process. It helps you to release any reservations you may have about making a change, like quitting smoking or changing your direction in any area of your life. It also helps you to extend your awareness into the future and visualize your lasting success.

4. **Getting Thru To Others:** We have included a chapter on our approach to relationships, because they are so closely connected with our problems. We include suggestions on how you can improve your relationships using the techniques described in this book.

5. **The Reframing Process:** This guided visualization process helps you to change any painful memory or image that goes through your mind. Based on the idea that "What you see is what you get," you may want to change some of the pictures you see. In a few minutes, you can transform a negative image into a positive one.

Figure 2.3, "When to Use GTT," provides a guide for using each of the Getting Thru Techniques.

Part 4:
Getting Down to Specifics

Part 4 provides specific applications for the techniques you will learn in Parts 2 and 3. We include some of the most common issues people face in our society, including:

1. Eliminating Stress

2. Overcoming Insomnia

3. Relieving Pain

FIGURE 2.3
WHEN TO USE GTT

The Getting Thru Techniques (GTT) include the use of EFT and provide a deeper level of understanding and healing than EFT alone. You can use GTT as a starting point or if you are not having the success you want with EFT alone.

PROCESS	RECOMMENDED USE
The Holistic Process	If EFT alone is not providing the results you want, or if you want to understand the problem at a deeper level, try this procedure. It can provide a deeper understanding of any issue, along with a deeper level of healing. This process, which includes the use of the EFT sequences, almost always helps. It is particularly effective with physical problems, as it helps to identify the emotional, mental and spiritual components of the problem.
The Unification Process	This process provides a deeper level of healing than the Holistic Process and includes the use of visualization. It is particularly helpful in providing images that you can use to assist yourself in the future and to monitor the healing process.
The Breakthru Process	This process can help you to make the decision to break through limitations that have been preventing you from achieving what you want in any aspect of your life. You need to use the Unification Process first.
The Reframing Process	This process helps to change any negative memory or image that runs through your mind to a positive one. It is particularly useful for changing painful images related to death or difficult experiences.

4. Creating Physical Well-being

5. Stopping Smoking and Other Habits

6. Reaching Your Ideal Weight

7. Increasing Physical Activity and Performance

8. Achieving Genuine Freedom

These chapters will help you to customize the EFT and GTT procedures for specific applications. You will also be able to understand specific problems you are dealing with. By the time you finish Part 4, you should have enough information to use EFT and GTT effectively in all aspects of your life. We also hope to expand your ideas of what you can achieve along the way, and to have you on the road to transforming your life into one filled with more and more joy, love, and freedom.

MORE HELP WITH GETTING THRU

In our descriptions of the techniques in this book, we have tried to be thorough and to provide as much information as we can put into words. Some people may understand the techniques better by seeing and hearing them in action, so we have also produced two video tapes and two audio cassette tapes to accompany this book.

The Video Tapes

On the videos, we demonstrate each of the techniques, using real life examples of EFT and GTT in action. These tapes help to clarify the locations of tapping points, positions for muscle testing, and the nuts and bolts of each of the processes. We highly recommend them to anyone who is interested in mastering EFT and GTT.

The Audio Tapes

The audio tapes are guided versions of the Getting Thru Techniques that allow you to relax and experience the processes. They include background music. Some people find listening to the descriptions of the processes easier than reading their way through them, as you do with the book alone.

There is more information about the videos and audio tapes in Appendix B.

CHAPTER THREE

Getting the Most from Your Mind

Knowing others is wisdom,
knowing yourself is enlightenment.

- LAO-TZU

In the last chapter, we provided an overview of the four levels of our energetic makeup – physical, emotional, mental and spiritual (PEM&S). Interestingly, the judgments, limiting beliefs, and unresolved emotions we found on these levels are also reflected in corresponding parts of the mind, in its reactions, and in the messages it sends to the body. Where there are blockages in the energy system, there is a higher degree of unconscious activity in the mind. Ultimately, this unconscious activity is what prevents us from moving toward achieving our full potential in life. It is also within the mind that we understand and integrate the changes we make with EFT and GTT.

In his book *Brain States*, Tom Kenyon divides the mind into four interconnected parts. Each has a specific function and corresponds psychologically to the four levels we have described in the energy field. This organizational system includes three parts of the physical brain and one non-physical part. The etheric (physical) level of the energy field roughly corresponds to the Reptilian brain, which relates primarily to the survival of the body. The emotional level corresponds to the Paleomallian brain, which includes parts of the brain related to the emotions along with many of the automatic functions of the body. The mental level corresponds to the Neomallian brain, which is associated with higher mammals and involves thought processes, reasoning, and language.

From the perspective of the energy system, the spiritual level is particularly interesting. The spiritual level corresponds to what Tom Kenyon calls the Mind, which has no physical location. This level has to do with our conscious awareness and memory. Kenyon notes that researchers have not been able to find a location in the physical brain that is responsible for storage of long-term memory. In fact, studies have shown that it is possible to remove large parts of the brain without affecting long-term memory in any way. The implication is that it is not housed within the physical brain. Instead, it is a function of the multi-dimensional aspects of the human energy system.

THE MYSTERIES OF THE MIND

Why is it important to explore the hidden recesses of the mind? Just look at what is happening in our lives. As mentioned previously, most of us know what is working and what is not working in our lives, but we usually do not know why.

For example, you may know that you are not attracting all of the money you would like to live a life filled with joy, love, and freedom, but you may not understand why. Or you may know that you sometimes become angry or fearful, but you do not know why. This lack of awareness seems to be the normal human condition.

As we begin to explore our inner world and examine "stuck" energy patterns, we are entering the realms of the unconscious mind. Through the connections between the energy system and the body, EFT and GTT release unconscious patterns that have become lodged in the mind. As we mentioned earlier, these unconscious patterns reflect blockages in the energetic flow in the meridian system. Multi-dimensionally, these patterns also reflect blockages in the energy field that surrounds the physical body.

The success of EFT has shown that when we are able to release blockages in the meridian system, they are also released in the mind, along with the more subtle levels of the energy field.

From this perspective, the meridian system becomes the interface between the physical body and the energy field.

As human beings, we have a wide range of thoughts and feelings. Ideally, we want joy, love, and freedom. But life is not always easy, and emotions like anger, fear, or grief serve a useful purpose. In fact, they are healthy when you experience them as momentary responses to the events in your life. For instance, expressing anger may be appropriate when another person is disrespectful or takes advantage of you. When faced with aggressive behavior, anger provides a way for you to express your disapproval and set clear boundaries for yourself.

Fear is a useful response when there is imminent danger.

Without it, your chance of survival may be limited. Fear stimulates the fight or flight mechanism, which gives you extra energy to remove yourself from the dangerous situation. And grief is an appropriate response when someone close has just died or left your life. In each of these cases, a healthy response is to express the emotions and release them, allowing you to return quickly to an experience of joy, love, and freedom.

Unfortunately, most of us are not able to release emotions this easily. Without knowing how to express them in a healthy way and create suitable boundaries for ourselves, emotions become stuck and frequently repressed. These emotions create imbalance in different aspects of our lives.

This imbalance usually occurs as the result of difficult or traumatic situations, along with programming we received as children and, to a lesser degree, as adults. Whenever we are unable to express our emotions and release them as they come up, they stay with us. Consequently, many adults are emotionally like little children, who are trying to deal with a harsh and complex world they do not understand.

You could compare the unresolved emotions we carry around with us to wads of trash that we throw over our shoulders on the road of life. We hope they will disappear behind us in the distance as we move forward. But the trash doesn't disappear. The unconscious mind is very efficient. It faithfully collects all of the trash we discard and saves each piece. It records all of our experiences much like a computer, and stores the emotions in its memory banks until we are able to deal with them.

Without attention, we end up with an unconscious mind that is full of trash. All of it takes energy to store and carry with us through our lives. In fact, much of our creative energy may be spent maintaining the trash heap in the unconscious mind rather than in creating a joyful life for ourselves. Like a computer, the mind also creates programs based on the input it receives. Our programming is composed of the unconscious responses our minds develop to deal with the situations that come up. If we are not in touch with the unconscious, it bases its reactions on these traumatic experiences and ideas we have picked up from the influential people in our lives.

Here are two examples of how the programming is created. The first relates to abundance, which is an issue for many people. Imagine a child named Joe whose father gives him a weekly allowance. Each week the father says something like this: "Be careful with this money – you know, it doesn't grow on trees. When you grow up you are going to have to work hard for every penny you earn." Then he begrudgingly hands the money to the child.

As an adult, how will Joe relate to money? Most likely, his unconscious mind will take his father's words literally, and he will have to work hard for every penny he earns. He probably will not know why it is so hard to keep up with his bills, and why he is always afraid of falling behind. If, on the other hand, he becomes aware that he is being limited by the programming in his unconscious mind, he can release the blockages and expand his possibilities.

Another example is a frail little girl we will call Julia, who is continuously belittled by a larger girl in her class. Regardless of how humiliated she feels, Julia has to go to school every day and hear more insults. She feels fear, resentment, and powerless in controlling the events of her life. And unless Julia has a way to release these emotions and beliefs, she will probably carry the fear, resentment, and powerlessness into adulthood, where they may prevent her from creating the joyful life she wants for herself. If she is able to release the limitations, she can move forward in a more powerful and productive way.

Can you think of some examples in your own life and the lives of those you know? There are probably many experiences that created your programming that you have forgotten entirely. Most people have a lot of stuck emotions, which means that their lives are ruled largely by the unconscious mind. We are like computers that are running on automatic. We are out of control and badly in need of reprogramming.

ENLISTING ALL OF YOUR RESOURCES

As we have seen with Joe and Julia, the most common reason we are unable to achieve what we want is simply that the unconscious mind has been programmed unproductively.

When you understand how the mind works, you have the ability to improve virtually any aspect of your life.

With EFT and GTT, we can tap into the immense resources of the unconscious and make tremendous changes in our lives. As Figure 2.1 explains, we can then turn our unresolved emotions into joy, our limiting beliefs into freedom, and our judgments into a life filled with love.

Most of us are unaware of the vast resources we have within us. We do not realize that the "I," or conscious mind, which we normally identify with, is just a minute part of the totality of who we are. We could compare the conscious mind to the tip of an iceberg, with a small point protruding above the surface of the water. Unknown to the casual observer, there is a huge expanse of ice beneath the surface that is hidden from view. Our mind is much the same. The conscious mind is about 10 percent; the remaining 90 percent is below the surface in what is commonly known as the subconscious or unconscious.

If we begin to bring awareness to the programming in the unconscious mind and bring it into alignment with the understanding of the Soul, we can take control of our lives and create what we truly desire. Tapping into the unconscious requires reaching with awareness below the surface thoughts that occupy our minds most of the time.

Usually our minds are running out of control. We talk to ourselves, sending messages to our unconscious minds about how poorly we are doing in school, how bad we look, how no one likes us, how poor our health is, how our back aches and on and on. When we are not blaming ourselves, we often blame others. And our unconscious mind dutifully records everything we say. We are continually programming ourselves with the things we tell ourselves. To this we add the input we receive from others, who may be unaware of the affect they are having on us. These other people are often simply replaying negative programs from their own unconscious minds.

With EFT and GTT, you now have the opportunity to consciously control the direction in which your life is going.

You can learn to program yourself productively and to eliminate undesirable old patterns. As you prepare to explore EFT, you may want to start this way. Buy a notebook to use as a journal, and make a list of any emotions you are dealing with that are preventing you from experiencing joy, love, and freedom in all aspects of your life. This will give you a place to begin with EFT.

Part 2

MASTERING THE EMOTIONAL FREEDOM TECHNIQUES

CHAPTER FOUR

The Basic EFT Sequences

*We would accomplish many more things
if we did not think of them as impossible.*

- C. MALESHERBEZ

Now the magic begins, using the EFT processes. We could recount dozens of stories about dramatic changes our students and clients have experienced. Phillip also used it with his younger students in the group home where he taught for many years. This is a home for severely emotionally-disturbed teenage boys who have not been able to function in the normal school system.

One of the main reasons they are in this setting is to learn to get along with others. One boy, whom we will call Jerome, came to the group home from Juvenile Hall because of drug abuse and criminal behavior. Despite his own shortcomings, Jerome protested loudly about being around some of the other boys, who were also there because of criminal offenses. He considered his classmates unforgivable, and felt that they should be severely punished.

By the end of the first week, Jerome completely refused to participate in the class, choosing to stay in a secluded time-out area. He wanted to transfer out of the school, even if it meant returning to Juvenile Hall. Phillip decided to have a talk with Jerome, hoping the boy would gain some insights into his judgmental behavior. He tried to help Jerome distinguish between a person's actions and his or her value as a person.

After listening to Jerome, Phillip introduced him to EFT. The emotion Jerome chose to clear was the hatred he felt toward his classmates, which he described as unbearably high. After a few rounds of EFT, Jerome said he felt better. Phillip also noticed that the boy's body, tone of voice, and breathing were more relaxed.

The weekend passed, and on Monday, Jerome was back in class. Phillip noticed that he was much friendlier toward his peers. After their softball practice, Jerome came over to Phillip and told him that his unbearable hatred toward the other boys was completely gone. He felt optimistic about being in the school and about his future. Jerome even mentioned that he had been practicing EFT on his own over the weekend and felt it really helped. This extraordinary turn-around could have a dramatic impact on this child's future.

Fortunately, you do not have to do EFT perfectly for it to work.

Jerome began to experience success with EFT after only fifteen minutes of assistance. He continued to use EFT on his own and got along better from then on.

You will be asked to tap approximately seven times on each point, but you don't have to keep an exact count. Anywhere between five and ten is usually fine. People often get good results even when they are not tapping exactly on the right acupuncture points. Nonetheless, we will try to describe the points clearly enough for you to be able to locate them precisely.

EFT includes a series of techniques that work like a team, and you may need to use more than one to achieve results. You may also have to repeat the procedure more than once to clear an emotional pattern completely. Using any technique or repetition of the process only takes a minute or two. With experience, you can release even a complex emotional pattern in a relatively short time.

THE POWER OF YOUR INTENT

One principle, which we will illustrate in Appendix A, is the power of your intent. This may explain why users are able to be effective with EFT even if they are not tapping exactly on the right points. If they intend to tap in the right place and to clear the blockage, then that is what occurs.

For this reason, we recommend that you have a sincere desire to clear a specific pattern as you perform the EFT sequences on yourself. Similarly, if you are assisting another person with EFT, your intent to help him or her to clear a blockage may influence the result positively. While we usually allow other people to tap on their own points, we often tap on ours at the same time with the intention of helping them to clear the blockage in their energy system.

On the other hand, loss of focus can reduce the effectiveness of the tapping procedures. While using EFT, you must keep your attention on what you are doing and the emotional blockage you intend to clear with the tapping. As we mentioned in Part 1, you need to have the disruption in place in the energy system when you do the tapping. This is done by focusing on the issue you intend to clear. If you want to clear a fear of public speaking, but think about relaxing on the beach in Hawaii while you perform the tapping sequence, you will confirm that you had a good time in Hawaii. But, when you finish, you will still be afraid of speaking in public.

To help you maintain your focus throughout the procedure, you will be asked to repeat a "reminder phrase" at each tapping point. This phrase identifies the emotion you are clearing as you tap, and reminds the unconscious mind that you are working with a specific blockage.

THE SHORT SEQUENCE

EFT revolves around the use of two simple tapping sequences. We use the first one, the Short Sequence, as the starting point for all of our EFT clearing work. Once you identify the pattern you want to release, it takes less than a minute to complete the Short Sequence. There is a summary of the steps in this process in Figure 4.1 and an illustration showing the locations of the tapping points in Figure 4.2.

We will break down the steps in the procedure here, because there are some subtleties that can affect your success. It is a simple process, but, as we mentioned before, it requires your complete attention.

Step 1: The Setup

To begin, it is important to understand that EFT works with specific emotions. While you will probably receive results over time applying EFT to a general subject like self-image, it is best to be specific. The setup identifies an emotion to clear.

Similarly, using EFT on physical symptoms is often more effective if you can identify the emotion(s) related to the condition. You will learn how to do this in Part 3, where we explore the Getting Thru Techniques. In the meantime, you can experiment with using EFT with the physical symptoms. This sometimes works. If not, you will have an opportunity to take your healing process to a deeper level with GTT when you have mastered the techniques in this part of the book.

Your Emotional Forest

You could compare your emotional world to a forest of trees. In this forest, each tree represents a specific emotional blockage in the meridian system. Most of us have a lot of them and find that it is very difficult to get anywhere in life without bumping into a lot of trees. Each tree also corresponds to an unresolved pattern in the unconscious mind; so each one is connected with a specific emotional experience or piece of programming.

The goal of EFT is to move freely wherever you want to go. Eventually, you may want to clear the entire forest to create a life filled with joy, love, and freedom. As Gary Craig says; "Every toppled tree represents another degree of emotional freedom."

We realize that cutting down trees is not an ecologically-sound idea, and it may actually be more accurate to make it a forest of billboard signs, which most of us want to eliminate. In this forest, each sign has the name of a specific emotional experience on it. Some of the billboards may read: "Fear I experienced when the neighbor's dog bit me when I was four;"

FIGURE 4.1
THE SHORT SEQUENCE

1. **THE SETUP:** Focus on bringing an emotion or issue into your awareness in the present moment. The key to the success of this process is to feel the emotion and set up the disruption in the meridian system.

2. **THE EVALUATION:** When you have brought the emotion up to its full intensity (or whatever intensity feels comfortable), measure how strong it feels between one and ten.

3. **THE AFFIRMATION:** While rubbing the "Sore Spot" on the chest (see the diagram in Figure 4.2 for location) in a circular fashion, repeat the following affirmation three times: "Even though I have this _____, I deeply and completely accept myself."

   Note: If you cannot rub the "Sore Spot", you can tap continuously on the "Karate Chop Spot" instead, while repeating the affirmation.

4. **THE TAPPING SEQUENCE:** Using your index and middle fingers, tap with a medium pressure about seven times on each of acupuncture points in the order shown on the diagram while repeating the following reminder phrase once at each point: "This _____."

   Note: You can tap on the points on either side. It doesn't matter which you use.

5. **THE RE-EVALUATION:** When you have completed the tapping sequence, take a moment to focus on the emotion or issue again and notice how it feels. Evaluate it again between one and ten to bring any difference in your experience into your awareness.

FIGURE 4.2
TAPPING POINTS FOR THE SHORT SEQUENCE

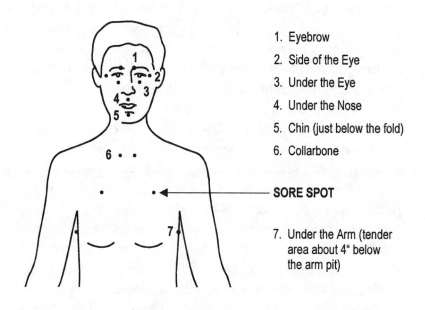

1. Eyebrow
2. Side of the Eye
3. Under the Eye
4. Under the Nose
5. Chin (just below the fold)
6. Collarbone

SORE SPOT

7. Under the Arm (tender area about 4" below the arm pit)

"Anger I experienced, because my father called me a 'little brat' throughout my childhood;" "Hostility I experienced toward my employer who belittled me in front of my peers when I was 27." With EFT, you do not need to identify the experience that created each emotion, but you do need to identify the emotion.

Aspects

With any emotional pattern, there are one or more trees. Each tree is called an "aspect." In a case like fear from a dog biting you at the age of four, there may be only one aspect, and one round of the process may completely clear the blockage. This is often true for phobic responses, which may be the result of a single highly traumatic experience. In other cases, there may be a whole grove of trees associated with a single emotion. For example, a child who was belittled by his father over a period of 10 years may have 100 aspects that are associated with the anger, fear, and resentment he felt and has carried with him into adulthood. If each round of the process removes one aspect or one tree, you may think that he will need to do the procedure 100 times to achieve results. Fortunately, this is not the case. Each time you do the process, you remove one tree, and the rest of the trees in the grove become shorter.

One hundred aspects is an extreme example, but after a few rounds of EFT, the anger will generally be noticeably reduced as all of the trees become shorter, and the entire pattern may clear with as little as ten rounds. This is known as the "generalization effect," because the process starts to generalize through all aspects of a complex problem after a few rounds. It also begins to generalize over the entire forest as you continue to use EFT, so improvements in one or two areas of your life will eventually produce improvement throughout, allowing you to experience the true power of emotional freedom.

With an understanding of aspects, you can see why even very intense emotions that have been with you for a long time may release quickly. It is really a matter of how many aspects are involved rather than how long you have had the problem or how intense it feels. This also demonstrates the value of persistence. If a pattern does not clear immediately, stay with it. You need to allow time for all of the aspects to be cleared, so that you can achieve complete relief.

Multiple Emotions

From our experience, most patterns clear completely within about one to six rounds. An emotion may also change after doing one or two rounds. For example a person may start with sadness, and after a round or two, experience anger. This means that anger is another aspect of the problem that was hidden under the sadness. With each round, you need to review the quality of the emotion and determine if it is actually the same one you felt before. And, as previously mentioned, you do not have to know where the emotion came from to use EFT effectively, but it is common for a greater awareness to come through while doing the procedure.

You may also start the process with more than one emotion related to a single problem. When this happens, decide which one is strongest and start there. If none is strongest, just start anywhere. Any related emotions will probably surface again later or may be cleared along with the strongest one.

One of the best things about using EFT is that it is gentle. If an emotion is painful, you do not have to bring it up to its highest intensity to be successful. It is necessary to focus on the issue to have the disruption in place in the energy system, but not to torture yourself. You may intentionally distance yourself from the emotion by imagining that there is a veil between you and the emotion, or by imagining that the emotion is a distance away from you.

There may also be times when you are not able to bring an emotion to the surface. You may know that an emotion is a problem for you, but you are not feeling it right now. When this happens, we recommend focusing on a time in the past when you felt the emotion. You can close your eyes for a moment and visualize the scene you were in when you had the emotion. Focus on feeling the emotions you felt then. This will generally bring the emotion to the surface so that you can clear the blockage with EFT.

The next step after you bring the emotion up is to identify it verbally in simple terms that you can use during the procedure. This is generally easy for emotions like anger and fear, but there may be times when you cannot identify an emotion. Some seem to defy precise descriptions and can only be suggested. For others, you just might not have the right word available. In this case, just call it whatever it feels like to you, like "this icky feeling," "this dumb emotion," or "this hollowness." All that matters is that you know what you are identifying, so when you describe it you send a clear message to your unconscious mind about what you intend to clear. For those who want a little help, you will also find a "Feelings Inventory" in Figure 4.3.

Step 2: The Evaluation

Before you start tapping, you have to measure the intensity of the emotion between one and ten, where one is the lowest

FIGURE 4.3
FEELINGS INVENTORY

AFRAID	ANGRY	HURT	POWERLESS
Awed	Annoyed	Aching	Depressed
Appalled	Bitter	Afflicted	Disbelieving
Awkward	Boiling	Agonized	Empty
Cowardly	Cross	Crushed	Exhausted
Dismayed	Enflamed	Despairing	Failing
Doubtful	Enraged	Distressed	Frustrated
Fearful	Fuming	Hapless	Guilty
Frightened	Incensed	Heartbroken	Helpless
Isolated	Indignant	Injured	Hopeless
Lonely	Infuriated	Mournful	Isolated
Menaced	Irritated	Offended	Lethargic
Out of place	Offended	Pained	Longing
Panicked	Provoked	Piteous	Numb
Quaking	Resentful	Sad	Regretful
Restless	Stewing	Suffering	Restless
Shaky	Sulky	Tortured	Shamed
Timid	Worked up	Victimized	Shocked
Threatened	Wrathful	Vulnerable	Sorrowful
		Worried	Tearful

intensity imaginable and ten is the highest. The goal of the process is to bring the intensity down to zero, where there is no remaining trace of the feeling. You need to quantify how strong the emotion is in the present moment, not the intensity you experienced last week or last year, or the intensity you imagine you might experience some time in the future. As a note, you can measure the intensity of physical symptoms in a similar way.

The SUD Level

This rating number is often called the SUD level, a handy psychological term which stands for "subjective unit of distress." Identifying the SUD level is a key part of the process, because it provides data that you can use to evaluate your progress and ultimate success. If you are not sure where the intensity is between one and ten, just guess. With experience, your confidence and accuracy will improve. We are even pretty successful at estimating the intensity of other people's emotions.

If you cannot even guess the intensity, or if you are dealing with something you cannot quantify, don't let that stop you. Just make note of how you feel, so you can compare it to how you feel after you finish the procedure. Your ability to identify the intensity will improve over time.

The Apex Problem

Why is identifying the SUD level is so important? Dr. Callahan identified an interesting phenomenon connected with TFT, which we have also noticed with our clients. He calls it the "apex problem." It is a form of denial that people often experience when doing subtle energy work. A problem may be very difficult when they begin, but, by the time the process is complete, they have forgotten how difficult it was before. They simply cannot believe the technique could produce such a profound transformation.

Many people come to us in great distress and leave feeling wonderful. You would think this would register as a success, but it is not so easy for the rational mind, which does not understand subtle energy. The rational mind wants tangible data and scientific proof. After experiencing a tremendous release, we have asked clients how things have changed only to find they can hardly recall having their original problem. Their rational minds cannot believe that this type of change is possible, so they go into a state of denial.

Quantifying the intensity of the emotion provides data for the rational mind to evaluate and brings more focus to the process. It is similar to medical test data. We all know that normal body temperature is 98.6. If you have a temperature of 104, you know that you are very ill. When it gets back below 100 you are getting better, and when it is back at 98.6, you are doing quite well. We measure blood pressure, cholesterol counts, and other physical phenomena in similar ways. So why not measure emotional intensity?

Using a scale of zero to ten to quantify emotional intensity removes much of the mystery, helps us to determine how to proceed, and measures the success of the process. Understanding this success then helps in the integration process. With awareness of the change that occurred, the recipient also comes to a deeper understanding of him or herself.

Some intellectually-oriented people have trouble distinguishing their emotions from their thoughts. These people may need more time and assistance with identifying their feelings and issues.

The Limits of the Rational Mind

Some people have a hard time crediting the success they experience to EFT. Their rational minds have to come up with an interpretation that fits their beliefs. Here are some common explanations for the positive changes people observe during demonstrations of the techniques at Gary Craig's seminars:

* They were hypnotized.

* It was positive thinking.

* They just wanted to get over their problems.

* They were distracted by all of the tapping.

* Whatever happened, it would not last, because there is no quick fix.

These reactions may seem a bit absurd, but they are common. If EFT's success is just a matter of positive thinking or wanting to get over a problem, why didn't they do it before? Distraction is not a likely explanation either, with the Evaluation Process. Something else has changed. Nonetheless, we have to factor in the power of our beliefs. We draw our conclusions from the information we have available to us. If EFT does not fit within these beliefs, the mind tries to explain away what it sees as best it can.

Fortunately, regardless of what we believe, EFT works. People often make improvements in spite of their skepticism.

Step 3: The Affirmation

This step addresses any unconscious blockages that may prevent you from achieving results with EFT. This phenomenon is known among users of EFT as Psychological Reversal (PR). When you have a form of PR, nothing you do will change the problem. The disruption is firmly in place in the meridian system and secured with a padlock. From another perspective, Gary Craig compares it to having a battery in backwards. Your portable radio may have enough power, but it will never play music. In such cases, you may think you want to get rid of the problem, but something is unconsciously preventing you from succeeding.

We will explain PR in more detail in the next chapter. For now, you just need to know how to eliminate it. You eliminate PR by repeating an affirmation that releases judgments and limiting beliefs. We already discussed how judgment toward ourselves, along with limiting beliefs about what we can achieve, are at the root of our difficulties. Craig and Fowlie estimate psychological reversal is only present about 40 percent of the time. But, using the complete overhaul principle, they include a generalized affirmation in the Short Sequence that clears most forms of PR.

The affirmation is:

"Even though I have this _____,
I deeply and completely accept myself."

You fill in the blank with the specific emotion or problem you are aiming to clear. So you would say something like: "Even though I have this anger, I deeply and completely accept myself," or "Even though I have this fear of public speaking, I deeply and completely accept myself," or "Even though I have this yucky feeling, I deeply and completely accept myself." For a physical problem, you can say something like "Even though I have this headache, I deeply and completely accept myself." This personalizes the affirmation to match the emotion or problem you have quantified.

Repeat this statement aloud three times aloud with conviction, while rubbing continuously on the Sore Spot shown on Figure 4.2. You can locate this spot by starting at the collarbone, then moving your fingers down past the first rib a few inches from the center of the chest. In keeping with the name, the spot usually feels pretty tender to the touch.

If you have a medical reason for not rubbing on the Sore Spot, there is an alternative. You can tap continuously on the Karate Chop Spot shown on Figure 4.6 instead. This is the place where karate users chop pieces of wood in half with their bare hands. It is located on the side of the hand below the little finger, right around the middle of the fleshy part of the hand. The Karate Chop Spot is easier for many people to locate, but Craig and Fowlie have found rubbing the Sore Spot to be more effective, so we recommend using it whenever possible.

Repeating the affirmation statement with conviction is important, because you want to convince the unconscious mind to make a shift. If you are just repeating the words, you may miss out and the tapping may not work. You do not have to believe the statement, but you have to be willing to say it. By saying you accept yourself in spite of the problem, you are sending yourself a message: You honor yourself for who you are, and are willing to rise above any self-doubt that could prevent you from overcoming your problem.

If you are in a situation where you cannot say the affirmation aloud, you may want to try saying it quietly to yourself, while maintaining the same conviction. If this does not work, you may have to wait until you are in a place where you can speak freely.

As previously mentioned, we will explore PR and affirmations more in the next chapter. For now, it is sufficient to know that you are aiming to remove the lock that is holding the pattern in place, and you want to do it with conviction.

Step 4: The Tapping Sequence

You should start the tapping sequence immediately after completing the affirmation. The tapping is done by holding the index finger and middle finger of one hand together and tapping with the ends of these fingers on the points shown in Figure 4.2 in the order shown and described below.

As you tap on each point, you repeat a reminder phrase one time aloud. Repeating the reminder phrase helps you to stay focused on the issue you want to clear and sends a continuing message of your intent to your unconscious mind. The reminder phrase is "This _____," filling in the blank with the same name you used in the blank for the affirmation.

If the affirmation was "Even though I have this grief, I deeply and completely accept myself," the reminder phrase is "This grief." You simply say "This grief" as you tap approximately seven times, repeating it once at each point. As we mentioned previously, you do not have to tap exactly seven times for the procedure to work. Anything between five and ten taps is fine.

For the points that are on both sides of the body, you can tap on either side. Jane's first reaction when she started using EFT was that if one side is good, two sides must be better. Nonetheless, we have not noticed any differences between tapping on one side or the other or both sides at once. You need to tap hard enough to send some energy through the meridians, but the tapping should not be painful. In this regard, tapping with the ends rather than the pads of the fingers seems to be most effective.

The tapping points are acupuncture points, so they are generally tender to the touch. When you tap on one directly, the spot is generally more sensitive than the area around it. This sensitivity should help you to locate the points. We can also describe their locations a little more precisely, and recommend familiarizing yourself with the locations before you attempt to go through the sequence.

1. **Eyebrow:** This point is at the inside edge of the eyebrow, above the inside corner of the eye.

2. **Side of the Eye:** This point is next to the outside of the eye, on the temple.

3. **Under the Eye:** This point is just below the middle of the eye, near the edge of the bone.

4. **Under the Nose:** This point is in the indentation just between the middle of the nose and the middle of the upper lip.

5. **Chin:** This point is on the middle of the chin, just below the crease.

6. **Collarbone:** This point is one of the trickier ones to locate. It is a tender area close to the end of the collar bone, next to the u-shaped indentation below the neck, just under the bone.

7. **Under the Arm:** This point is in the tender area on the side of the chest about four inches below the armpit.

Step 5: The Re-evaluation

When you finish the tapping, take a nice, deep breath and allow the energy to settle for a moment. You may also notice yourself automatically taking a deep breath during the procedure. This is a normal release, and it helps to allow your self to breathe deeply.

The Power of the Breath

Most people think of the breath just as a way to move air in and out of the lungs.

Breathing can be a powerful way to move energy around in the body and to break up energetic congestion.

While you continue reading, you might want to take a couple of deep breaths and notice how you feel when you are done. Simply closing your eyes for a moment and taking a few nice deep breaths can completely change your frame of mind. With your intent, you can also direct energy into different areas of the body as you inhale, releasing stuck energy as you exhale. This is a great way to release tension, clear your mind, and energize yourself.

Some people also feel physical sensations as the energy within and around them reconfigures itself. You may want to wait a moment before proceeding, if you are feeling the energy shift. This will help you to integrate the shift.

Once you feel settled, you are ready to re-evaluate. Return to focusing on the original emotion or issue, like you did at the beginning of the procedure. Measure the intensity between zero and ten, and compare it with the original intensity. In most cases, there is a significant difference. The emotion may be completely gone. If not, the important thing to note is the difference. It generally takes more than one round of the process to release an emotion completely. These are the possibilities to consider:

1. **Partial Relief:** The intensity of the emotion is lower than when you started, but it is still above a two in intensity. This means that there is another aspect of the emotion or issue to examine. The next step is to repeat the Short Sequence to clear the remaining emotions.

2. **Nearly Complete Relief:** The intensity of the emotion is down to two or less, so there is just a small residue left. In most cases, this residue will release with a short process called the Floor-to-Ceiling Eye Roll. Try this one next. If the emotion clears, you are done. If not, repeat the Short Sequence.

3. **Complete Relief:** The intensity is gone completely. In this case, focus on being in a situation you are likely to experience in the future that would previously have triggered the emotion or issue. Imagine yourself there to see if you get any emotional intensity. If you do, you can repeat the Short Sequence to clear the remaining intensity. If you cannot come up with any intensity, the pattern may be completely gone.

4. **Little or No Relief:** The emotional intensity has not changed, or you have completed several rounds and the intensity has not changed much. When this happens, we recommend using the Complete Sequence, which is described later in this chapter.

When a pattern has cleared completely, you might want to take a moment to reflect on what has changed. People often experience a new sense of peace and calmness. We already discussed how the unconscious trash we carry with us takes energy to maintain. It follows that when it is gone there is often a feeling of being lighter, calmer, and more present. When a blockage is removed, it allows you to be comfortable with yourself and to more fully experience the present moment. You may also have a new understanding of what has happened, including where the emotion or issue came from and the freedom you have achieved by releasing it. Enjoy these times and write your understandings in your journal.

There is no way of knowing whether an emotion will return or not. If it surfaces in the future, you can simply repeat the process. In any case, the clearing you have done has moved you closer to achieving emotional freedom.

Repeating the Short Sequence

If you have achieved partial relief after completing the Short Sequence, you are ready to repeat the process. When you evaluate the intensity of the emotion or issue again in Step 2, notice if it feels the same or if it has shifted to another emotion or issue. Physical symptoms may even move around in the body. This is positive. It means that they are releasing.

If what you are experiencing has changed, you can work on the new issue in the same way as the original one. Complex patterns with a lot of aspects may have a several different emotions connected with them. Moving from one to the next is an indication that you are making progress. You are removing the trees from the grove one by one. The key is just to continue tapping your way through the emotions that come up.

If you do not notice any difference in the quality of the emotion other than intensity, you can repeat the procedure with the same emotion. In this case, you need to distinguish it from the disruption you cleared in the first round by calling it something slightly different like "This remaining _____." If you said "This fear" the first time, call it "This remaining fear" the second time. When you repeat the affirmation, then you will say something like:

- "Even though I still have some of this _____, I deeply and completely accept myself."

  or

- "Even though I have this remaining _____, I deeply and completely accept myself."

The reminder phrase will be:

- "This remaining _____."

Each time you repeat the process with the same emotion, you need to change the label slightly, with the understanding that each of the trees has a different label on it.

ESTELLE'S PROCESS: THE SHORT SEQUENCE AT WORK

Here is an example of the Short Sequence related to losing weight. EFT is very effective for dealing with food cravings and weight issues. We have found that an important key to permanent weight loss is addressing any emotions you have about your weight and feeling good about yourself regardless of what you weigh.

A woman whom we will call Estelle attended one of our workshops for help with her weight problem. She was kind enough to share her feelings with the class. When she focused on her weight, she remembered that her mother called her "fatso" when she was a girl. This made her feel bad about herself and depressed. She also felt sad and unloved. When she grew up and looked at pictures of herself as a child, she was surprised to see that she was not really overweight. Nonetheless, she had believed her mother's words and considered herself fat. Now as she was becoming older, her weight was creeping upward, and she wanted to bring it under control. We started the EFT by working with the depression, because that was the strongest emotion. Before the first round, her SUD level was an eight. We did a round of the Short Sequence, which brought it down to a five. Then we reviewed the quality of the emotion and realized that she was feeling anger toward her mother now. As we mentioned before, changing from one emotion to another is a common occurrence, as another aspect of the problem surfaces. It is also common for a person to experience sadness or depression as a way to deal with unresolved anger.

Since Estelle had made some progress using the Short Sequence in the first round, we decided to repeat it with the anger. Her SUD level for anger at this time was around six. After another round of EFT, the anger was down to zero.

With the anger gone, we reviewed the other emotions she started with: depression, sadness, feeling bad about herself, and feeling unloved. All of them were gone and she felt fine about herself, so the process was complete. It probably took less than ten minutes, and it effectively moved Estelle closer to her goal of controlling her weight.

We will discuss using EFT for food cravings and weight issues in more detail in Part 4 of this book.

THE FLOOR–TO-CEILING EYE ROLL

This short process is very simple and only takes a few seconds to complete. Use it whenever you have reduced the intensity of an issue to two or less with the Short or Complete Sequence, but have not quite reached zero.

First you have to locate the "Gamut Spot" on your hand. You will find the location for this point, along with a description of the process, in Figure 4.4. It is located on the back of the hand just below the space between the little finger and the ring finger, near the knuckles. To do this procedure, tap continuously on this point while focusing on the emotion and completing a simple eye exercise.

You do the eye exercise while holding your head facing straight ahead. Begin with your eyes looking down as low as possible. If you are sitting in a chair, you should be looking straight down at the floor. Start tapping continuously on the Gamut Spot, hold your head still, remind yourself of the emotion, and gradually move your gaze upward over a period of about six seconds until you are looking as high up as you can. Keep tapping continuously on the Gamut Spot until you finish. If you are sitting in a chair, you should be looking at the ceiling when you are done, and your head should be in its original position.

That is the entire process. When you are finished, take a nice deep breath. Then focus on the emotion again, like you did when you completed the tapping sequence. In most cases, it will be gone. If not, you can repeat the Short or Complete Sequence to clear the rest of the emotion.

THE COMPLETE SEQUENCE

This is the sequence we use for stubborn emotions, when the Short Sequence is providing no results or minimal results. It is summarized in Figure 4.5. This process includes more points in the tapping sequence. The tapping is also done twice with another technique called the Nine Gamut Process sandwiched in between.

FIGURE 4.4
THE FLOOR-TO-CEILING EYE ROLL

---

1. **THE EVALUATION:** Normally you will select this process after the Short Sequence or the Complete Sequence has brought the problem down to a one or two.

2. **THE TAPPING SEQUENCE:** Begin by holding your head facing straight ahead and tapping continuously on the Gamut Spot. Hold your head still. Now look down as far as you can toward the floor. While focusing on the problem and continuing to tap on the Gamut Point, gradually move your gaze upwards over a period of about six seconds until you are looking up as high as your eyes will go. While doing this, repeat once the reminder phrase you have chosen for the emotion: "This _____."

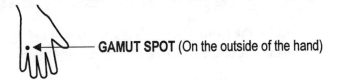

GAMUT SPOT (On the outside of the hand)

3. **THE RE-EVALUATION:** When you have completed the process, take a moment to focus on the emotion again and notice how it feels. Measure it again between one and ten. In most cases it will be gone. If this is not the case, you may want to continue with the Short Sequence or the Complete Sequence.

Steps 1, 2 and 3:
The Setup, Evaluation, and Affirmation

The Complete Sequence starts in the same way as the Short Sequence with the Setup, Evaluation, and Affirmation.

Step 4(A): The Long Tapping Sequence

Begin the tapping with the first seven points you covered in the Short Sequence, and continue with the following points on either of the hands. You will find the locations of these points in Figure 4.6.

8. **Outside of the Thumb:** This point is next to the fingernail.

9. **Side of the Index Finger:** This point is next to the fingernail on the side of the index finger facing the thumb.

10. **Side of the Middle Finger:** This point is next to the fingernail on the side of the middle finger facing the index finger.

11. **Side of the Little Finger:** This point is next to the fingernail on the side of the little finger facing the ring finger.

12. **The Karate Chop Spot:** This point is on the side of the hand below the little finger, in the middle of the fleshy part of the hand.

Step 4(B): The Nine Gamut Process

When you complete the long tapping sequence, you do a series of eye exercises that stimulate and balance the different parts of the brain. The purpose of this process is to activate all of your resources. As with the Floor-to-Ceiling Eye Roll, start

FIGURE 4.5
THE COMPLETE SEQUENCE

1. **THE SETUP:** Refer to Figure 4.1, "The Short Sequence."

2. **THE EVALUATION:** Refer to Figure 4.1.

3. **THE AFFIRMATION:** Refer to Figure 4.1.

4. **THE TAPPING SEQUENCES:** With the Complete Sequence, there are three separate parts.

   A. **THE LONG TAPPING SEQUENCE:** Using your index and middle fingers, tap with a medium pressure about seven times on each of the following meridian points, in the order shown on the Figure 4.6. Repeat the following reminder phrase aloud once at each point.: "This _____."

   B. **THE NINE GAMUT PROCESS:** While tapping continuously on the Gamut Spot, go through the following eye movements while holding your head straight forward:

      1. Close your eyes.
      2. Open your eyes.
      3. Look down hard to the right.
      4. Look down hard to the left.
      5. Roll your eyes around once in a clockwise circle.
      6. Roll your eyes around one in a counterclockwise circle.
      7. Hum for about two seconds from any song, like "Happy birthday to you ..."
      8. Count aloud from one to five.
      9. Repeat the humming.

   C. **THE LONG TAPPING SEQUENCE:** Repeat the tapping sequence from Part A of the process.

5. **THE RE-EVALUATION:** Refer to Figure 4.1.

FIGURE 4.6
TAPPING POINTS FOR THE COMPLETE SEQUENCE

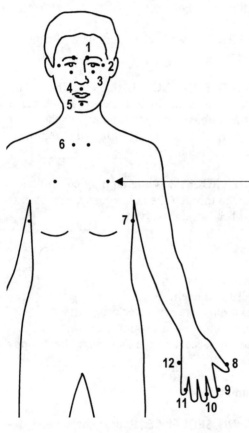

1. Eyebrow
2. Side of the Eye
3. Under the Eye
4. Under the Nose
5. Chin (just below the fold)
6. Collarbone

SORE SPOT

7. Under the Arm (tender area about 4" below the arm pit)
8. Outside of the Thumb
9. Side of the Index Finger
10. Side of the Middle Finger
11. Side of the Little Finger
12. Karate Chop Spot

with your head facing straight forward, and hold it in the same position during the entire process. You also tap continuously on the Gamut Spot through the entire procedure. Once you start tapping, go through the following sequence of exercises:

1. Close your eyes.
2. Open your eyes.
3. Look down hard to the right.
4. Look down hard to the left.
5. Roll your eyes around in a complete clockwise circle.
6. Roll your eyes around in a complete counterclockwise circle.
7. Hum aloud for about two seconds from any song like "Happy birthday to you ..."
8. Count aloud from one to five.
9. Repeat the humming for another two seconds.

According to Craig and Fowlie, you do not necessarily have to do the exercises in this order, but you do need to hum, count, and hum again in that order. You can mix up the rest, if you wish.

Step 4(C): The Long Tapping Sequence

Repeat the tapping sequence you went through in Step 4(A).

Step 5: The Re-Evaluation

Now you are at the end of the procedure. Take a nice deep breath like you did with the Short Sequence. Then focus again on the emotion and quantify the intensity between zero and ten. As with the Short Sequence, there are a few possibilities:

1. **Partial Relief:** The emotional intensity is lower than when you started, but it is still above a two. The next step is to repeat the Complete Sequence to clear the remaining intensity.

2. **Nearly Complete Relief:** The emotional intensity is down to two or less. Try the Floor-To Ceiling Eye Roll. If this clears the issue, you are done. If not, repeat the Complete Sequence.

3. **Total Relief:** The intensity is gone completely. In this case, we recommend focusing on being in a situation that you are likely to experience in the future that would normally trigger the pattern. Imagine yourself there to see if you get any emotional intensity. If you do, you can repeat the Short or Complete Sequence to clear the remaining emotions. If you cannot come up with any intensity, the pattern may be gone.

4. **Little or No Relief:** The intensity of the emotion has not changed. Or you have gone through a few rounds, and it is not changing very much. When this happens, try Kinesiology, which is described the next chapter, or the Collarbone Breathing Exercise, which is described in Chapter 6.

You may be wondering if thinking about the emotion is a good indication of what your response will be the next time you encounter it in real life. In most cases, the answer is yes. Take the example of the water phobia that Dr. Callahan cleared by tapping under his client's eye. When the woman with the phobia got close to water, she was still free of symptoms. Usually thinking about a situation that would trigger the emotion will produce the same reaction as being there. The unconscious mind does not know the difference between fantasy and reality. The exception would be if another aspect comes up when you get to the real life experience.

EXPERIMENTING WITH THE TAPPING SEQUENCES

With the sequences you have seen so far, you should be able to experience relief from most emotional difficulties. We suggest trying it for yourself and logging your results in your journal. Most people notice changes in their lives after addressing just one or two issues with EFT. If you practice on one new issue a day, you will be well on the way to making some dramatic changes in your life.

CHAPTER FIVE

Using Kinesiology with EFT

Men are not prisoners of fate,
but only prisoners of their own minds.

- FRANKLIN D. ROOSEVELT

Kinesiology (muscle testing) is a powerful way to access information from the unconscious mind and the body's innate intelligence. It works by testing how the strength of a muscle is affected by focusing on an external stimulus or a part of the body. With Kinesiology, you can test how the body is affected by the introduction of specific foods, vitamins, scents, music, environmental factors, and verbal statements. You can also test the strength of different systems in the body and its surrounding energetic structure.

With EFT, you may want to try Kinesiology if both the Short and Complete Sequence are providing little or no relief. Muscle testing will tell you if psychological reversal is blocking your success. It will give you more information about what is happening in your unconscious mind.

As mentioned, Kinesiology has many applications. It is not our intention to cover them all here. This chapter focuses on using it with EFT. If you want to know more about Kinesiology itself, refer to Appendix B, "Resources."

THE AFFECTS OF PSYCHOLOGICAL REVERSAL

In our discussion of holistic healing in Chapter Two, we explained how emotions are tied to limiting beliefs and judgments. Sometimes these beliefs and judgments are so strong that they need to be cleared before we can remove the emotional blockages. These forms of self-sabotage are what we call psychological reversal. We addressed this phenomenon in a general way with the affirmation in the EFT tapping sequences and will address it more specifically here. The use of Kinesiology can greatly enhance your success with EFT.

Most people have a moderate amount of PR. With these individuals, PR will show up in a few specific areas of their lives, but not in others. This means that some parts of their lives will work well, but other parts will not. The phrase "Lucky at cards, unlucky at love" is an example of this phenomenon, although luck has nothing to do with it. It is a matter of where the energy is flowing smoothly and where it is not. Where we have limiting beliefs and judgments about ourselves, the energy is not flowing smoothly. So when we examine PR, we are moving from the emotional level of healing to the mental and spiritual levels that we described in Figure 2.1.

There are also the rare individuals who have very little PR. They tend to recover from challenges quickly and easily. Others have a lot of it and almost always have difficulty overcoming the obstacles they face. This is also less common, but helpful to understand. In such cases, PR may show up with almost every problem they face.

We have already seen that PR is a polarity problem and not a character defect. It is just a matter of having your batteries in backward. Nonetheless, some conditions are frequently linked with it. Gary Craig has noticed that people who are prone to addictions, depression, or chronic diseases are almost always psychologically reversed in relation to these problems. PR is also linked with procrastination, negative thinking, learning difficulties, and problems with athletic performance. This seems logical, because all of these conditions are forms of self-sabotage. To the degree that you have such problems, you probably also have a corresponding inability to make positive changes in your life.

OVERCOMING PSYCHOLOGICAL REVERSAL

We have already used a general affirmation to correct PR. This affirmation works most of the time, but not always. When it does not work, the Short and Complete EFT Sequences do not work either, because the affirmation is not reaching the specific beliefs and judgments in the unconscious mind. In such cases, you need to deal with the reversal more specifically for EFT to be effective. This is the reason for using Kinesiology.

In its use with EFT, the goal of the muscle testing is to fine-tune the affirmation and effectively release the PR with the Short or Complete Sequence. The test statements used to determine the nature of PR are shown in Figure 5.1. Testing these statements with Kinesiology demonstrates how the unconscious mind develops ineffective strategies to cope with life's challenges. The test muscle will remain strong when

given a statement that agrees with your unconscious programming or a statement that is true to you. Testing the
statements in this figure will show you if there are any limiting
beliefs or judgments hat need to be cleared before a pattern
can be released.

You may be surprised at the results you get with Kinesiology. It can explain why you may be working hard to overcome
an obstacle and getting nowhere. Unconsciously, you probably
do not want to get over it or believe that you deserve to get over
it. These sabotaging strategies may include an inability or un-
willingness to overcome physical and/or emotional symptoms.
The mind may see the symptoms as a way to get attention, to
avoid unpleasant situations, or to protect you from danger.

Let us explain these examples. We all need to be nurtured
and loved, so we seek ways for this to occur. Some people are
unable to reach out to others and create mutually loving relationships, or find themselves alone. In such cases, they may
unconsciously manifest painful physical or psychological
symptoms as a way to get others to care for them. A doctor or
nurse's care is better than no care at all.

Illness is also a way to avoid stressful situations, such as
going to work or to school. And conditions like carrying extra
weight may provide protection for a person who feels unsafe
around other people, particularly the opposite sex. When this
is the case, the individual may work diligently to lose weight
with little or no success. These are just a few examples. The
possible interpretations of the unconscious mind are endless.

It follows that when the symptoms are providing a hidden
benefit, it is unlikely that EFT or any other clearing technique
will be successful. Using Kinesiology to muscle test the statement "I want to get over this _____" will often expose
this form of psychological reversal. If the muscle tests weak, it

---

FIGURE 5.1
THE LEVELS OF PSYCHOLOGICAL REVERSAL (PR)

When PR is present, one or more of the statements will probably produce a weak response with muscle testing:

- I want to get over this _____.
- I want to <u>completely</u> get over this _____.
- I <u>will</u> get over this _____.
- I believe that I can get over this _____.
- I deserve to get over this _____.

Here are a few more variations you can try:

- I will do all the things necessary to get over this _____.
- I will allow myself to get over this _____.
- It is possible for me to get over this _____.
- Getting over this _____ will be good for me.
- Getting over this _____ will be good for others.
- If will be safe for me to get over this _____.

When there is no PR, you will receive a strong response for all of these statements. To confirm your results, you can test the opposite statements. With no PR, they should all produce a weak response. With PR, the response should be strong for the following statements:

- I don't want to get over this _____.
- I don't want to <u>completely</u> get over this _____.
- I <u>won't</u> get over this _____.
- I don't believe I can get over this _____.
- I don't deserve to get over this _____.

---

means you do not want to get over it on an unconscious level. The statements "I want to completely get over this _____" and "I will get over this _____" are also helpful when a person is receiving partial success, but doesn't seem to be able to release a blockage completely.

With the understanding that a strong response means that a statement is true to your unconscious mind, a weak response means that the statement is false. If the muscle tests weak for any of these statements, your unconscious mind does not want to overcome the problem, and you need to eliminate the PR to make progress with EFT.

A common form of reversal has to do with belief in oneself. If a person is holding onto an unconscious belief that it is going to be difficult or impossible to release a blockage, or that it has to take a long time and include a lot of physical or emotional pain, her success with EFT may reflect this belief.

Another self-defeating pattern has to do with deserving to be better. If you are holding onto shame, believing that you are inherently bad or unworthy, your external reality will reflect this judgment. This is obviously inconvenient if you want to manifest abundance in your life, create a loving relationship, or move forward into a fulfilling career.

EXAMPLE: MELANIE'S PR

In one of our classes, Jane was working with a woman we will call Melanie, who was considering a career change and experiencing fear about her ability to succeed. They went through the Short Sequence together to release the fear and had some success, but Melanie was not able to bring the intensity down to zero. They went through several rounds of the process during which Melanie described her feelings. Jane could not help noticing that Melanie repeatedly mentioned how difficult the pattern was going to be to release.

When it became clear that Melanie was only achieving partial success, Jane did some muscle testing on Melanie to confirm her suspicions about the nature of the problem and to help her understand what was happening. Melanie tested strong (positive) for the statement "I want to get over this problem," but when Jane tested her for "I believe I can get over this problem," Melanie tested weak (negative). In her case, the solution was to change the affirmation used at the beginning of the EFT sequence to "Even though I don't believe I can get over this self-doubt, I deeply and completely accept myself." With that done, Melanie could release the remaining fear.

As mentioned before, Craig and Fowlie found that PR is present less than 40 percent of the time. This means that usually your beliefs and judgments are not going to prevent you from simply tapping the emotion away with EFT. They usually release along with the emotions. When they are locked in place, however, you need to be able to release them and move forward with your life.

Sometimes just saying the affirmation we used with the Short Sequence or the Complete Sequence will bring up more understanding of what is in the way. When this happens, you can tailor your affirmation to the exact nature of the belief or judgment you have encountered. If you do not know what the problem is, Kinesiology can help.

Kinesiology can uncover self-defeating patterns that may be blocking success with EFT. It also demonstrates how unconscious patterns influence the ability to recover.

And, in the spirit of EFT, testing for PR is relatively easy to do. It takes only a few minutes and can greatly enhance your success with EFT.

GETTING STARTED WITH KINESIOLOGY

You can use Kinesiology alone or with another person. We will describe ways to do both. Receiving accurate results requires focused awareness, some practice, and an ability to be neutral about the results. Both the provider and receiver need to be open to the information that is coming up from the unconscious without drawing any premature conclusions about the results. If you think you already know the outcome, your bias may influence the results.

For those who are inexperienced with Kinesiology, we recommend doing EFT to clear any doubts you may have about your ability to use muscle testing successfully. Many people become psychologically reversed when trying something new. EFT can help overcome any fear or anxiety you may have related to Kinesiology.

Preparation

Before testing with Kinesiology, we suggest the following:

1. Be sure the environment is neutral with no distracting music, scents, and so on.

2. If possible, have the person receiving the Kinesiology drink some water. This optimizes brain functioning.

3. Be in a neutral emotional state and centered. If you are working on another person, be sure that he or she is also in a centered state. The process we use follows.

4. If you are testing another person, only do so with his or her permission and understanding of the importance of being neutral.

THE CENTERING PROCESS

Before starting with Kinesiology and any other healing work, we use a short relaxation process to get ourselves centered and grounded, along with our clients and students. Centering yourself in this way brings you into a state of balance that facilitates any healing process.

Energetically, we normally see a lot of static around people, which comes from all of the energy they are exposed to throughout the day. Removing the static clears up the picture and facilitates the deeper healing work. Doing this process before muscle testing also brings you into a relaxed state of presence where you feel neutral and open to whatever the body may reveal.

We suggest something like the following script, which you can read slowly aloud or to yourself. It is most effective if you can close your eyes occasionally and focus your attention on your body. If you are reading the process to yourself, you may want to pause between sentences and close your eyes. Allow yourself to feel what is happening in your body, and to imagine the ball of energy that surrounds you and flows through you.

Take a few deep breaths. Imagine that you are breathing in clear, fresh air, and as you exhale that you are releasing any tension you are holding in your body. As you continue to focus on your breath, imagine that you are firmly grounded with a cord that extends from the base of your spine to the center of the earth and that you are surrounded by a ball of energy. Focus on re-

leasing with each exhale. Allow any tension you feel in your body to melt down the grounding cord and into the earth, where it can be easily absorbed, so you feel more relaxed with each breath.

Now imagine that the ball of energy around you extends at least a few feet on all sides – above you, below you, to both sides, to the front and in the back – so that you are completely surrounded and protected by it. Now ask any energy that is not your own to move out of this ball. We all pick up energetic debris as we go through our daily lives, just like a table top picks up dust. If you ask this energetic debris to leave, it will. Just take in a couple more breaths of that clear energy, and feel the debris drifting away, back to its source.

When this is done, ask to return all of your own energy to you. Just as we pick up energy from other people and places, we leave bits of our own energy wherever we go. Now you want to feel this energy returning to you, allowing you to feel whole and complete.

Now focus for a moment on bringing clear energy into your mind with each inhale, so that your entire brain feels clear, balanced, and alert. Feel this clear energy moving into both sides of your brain, so that your mind is balanced and so that any leftover thoughts from the day can drift off for now. Allow yourself to be here in this moment with a clear mind.

When you feel clear and relaxed, take another deep breath, bringing in clear focus to help you with the Kinesiology.

ARM TESTING WITH TWO PEOPLE

When you are centered, you are ready to start muscle testing. One of the easiest ways to use Kinesiology is with a partner. We suggest the following arm testing method:

1. **Position the Person to be Tested:** Have the person to be tested, whom we will call the receiver, stand erect, holding one

arm out straight to the side. The elbow and hand should be extended, so they form a straight line that is parallel with the floor, with the palm of the hand facing down. Either arm may be used for the testing, as long as it is in healthy condition. You should not perform this type of muscle testing on an area of the body with an injury.

2. **Position the Person Performing the Testing:** The person who is to perform the testing, the provider, then stands either in front of or behind the receiver, facing the extended arm. The provider places one hand on the receiver's shoulder for stability and the other hand on top of the extended arm, at the wrist, so the provider's hand is touching the wrist lightly, but not exerting any pressure. Placing the hand on the wrist before starting the testing allows the receiver to become accustomed to the touch.

3. **Review the Testing Procedure:** To test, the provider says a phrase for the receiver to repeat aloud, starting with "My name is _____." When the receiver has completed the statement, the provider pushes straight down on the extended arm, at the wrist. Here are a few tips.

   • Allow the receiver to complete the statement and push on the arm itself, not on the hand. If you push on the hand, you are actually testing the wrist, which is generally not strong enough for this type of test.

   • To be sure the receiver is paying attention, have the provider say "resist" just before exerting pressure on the arm.

   • Hold the hand that will be pushing flat, and push straight down with the palm, gradually increasing the pressure to test the resistance.

- Avoid any jerky or chopping movements or gripping on the receiver's arm.

4. **Test for accuracy:** The first few tests should be designed to determine the strength of the receiver's arm and the accuracy of the results. Start with the receiver's name, then test for another name and a few other easy questions, like the date, the location you are in, and so on. A true statement should generate a strong response and a false statement should generate a weak response. In addition to testing the accuracy of the results, the first few questions provide base data on the difference between a positive and negative response.

   If the receiver does not provide accurate results to the first few tests, do not proceed further until you have corrected the problem. There are a few things that may be happening:

   - The receiver may be dehydrated. Have him or her drink at least a full glass of water. Retest and proceed if the results are accurate.

   - The receiver may not be centered and grounded. Repeat the Centering Process to bring him or her back into the present moment. Retest and proceed if the results are accurate.

   - If you get an equally strong response when testing for the receiver's name and another name, the receiver may have Neurological Disorganization, which is described in the next chapter. Use this procedure for correcting this condition before proceeding further. Repeat the name test and proceed if the results are accurate.

5. **Test for PR:** With accurate results, you are ready to test anything you wish. For use with EFT, test "The Levels of Psychological Reversal" in Figure 5.1.

If you are new to muscle testing, we recommend starting with a partner and practicing arm testing until you feel competent. This is one of the easiest forms of muscle testing. Then you can move on to self-testing.

SELF-TESTING

Self-testing has some benefits. The most obvious is that you do not need to have another person around. As you develop your skills with muscle testing, you may also find it easier to test yourself, even when there is another person available. When you have fully developed your skills in muscle testing, the main reason to test other people is to show them the responses their bodies are providing. We have found that you can get the same information testing on yourself, even if you are testing for another person. This is called surrogate muscle testing. It is described in more detail in Appendix A.

The One-Hand Method

There are several ways to perform self-testing. We prefer the One-Hand Method, because it leaves the other hand free if you want to test a substance. We will discuss this more in the next chapter, where we explore energy toxins. Another advantage to this approach is its subtlety. You can do this without drawing attention to yourself, so you can use it anywhere. We use this form of muscle testing extensively in our consulting work to pinpoint the source of a problem, to determine which EFT procedure to use next, and so on. Here is our technique:

1. Hold one hand with the middle finger extended straight out from the hand. We generally recommend using your non-dominant hand, because this leaves your dominant hand free

to hold a substance you want to test, if desired.

2. With this method of self-testing, the middle finger serves the same purpose as the extended arm in arm testing, and the index finger corresponds to the hand of the provider who is exerting pressure on the arm. Hold the index finger over the middle finger, touching lightly.

3. Proceed with questions just as you would with arm testing, resisting with the middle finger and exerting pressure with the end of the index finger. This may take a bit of practice, but you can confirm the reliability of your results by testing a series of questions to which you know the answers and testing the responses you receive.

As a note: some people prefer to use the index finger as the extended arm and the middle finger to exert pressure. You can experiment with both and decide if either one feels comfortable to you. If not, your may prefer using two hands.

The Two-Hand Method

This is one of a number of ways to muscle test with two hands.

1. Hold the first hand out and form a loop with your thumb and index finger. This hand will be the equivalent to the extended arm. You can use either hand, but may prefer your non-dominant hand. With this method, you will test your ability to hold the thumb and finger of the first hand together.

2. Hold the thumb and index finger of your second hand together, and extend the fingers so that you can place them inside of the loop you have formed with the thumb and finger of the first hand. The thumb of the second hand should be touching the thumb of the first hand, and the index finger

should be touching the index finger of the first hand.

3. Proceed with questions just as you would with arm testing, resisting with the thumb and finger loop while you try to pull the loop apart with the thumb and finger of your second hand.

INTERPRETING YOUR RESULTS

Once you have completed the testing, you need to interpret the results. You are drawing information from the unconscious mind and the body's innate intelligence, so the results may not match the receiver's conscious intent, thoughts, or desires. A strong response to a question indicates that the statement is true to the receiver or that the condition described is understood as beneficial in the mind of the receiver. A weak response indicates that the statement is untrue to the receiver or that the condition described is not understood as beneficial to the receiver.

As previously mentioned, responses to statements like "I want to be successful in life," "I want to get over this fear," or "I want to be my ideal weight" are easy to understand. A strong response means this statement is true, and a weak response means this statement is false. Responses to other statements may be less obvious. The key is to remember that you are testing the response to whatever you are instructing the person to focus on.

Consider statements like "Think about anxiety" or "Think about your job." A strong response to thinking about anxiety or any other negative emotion means that the mind understands the emotion to be a positive thing. Similarly, a strong response to thinking about your job means that the mind responds positively to your job. It follows that if you have a positive response to the statement "Think about money," your mind views money as a positive thing. Surprisingly, many people test weak to this statement and strong to thinking about a variety of negative emotions.

The statements that draw a strong response show what we are attracting to ourselves. So if a person tests strong for anxiety and weak for money, he may not be able to create the kind of life he wants. This is why Kinesiology is so powerful. It is a way to find out what you are attracting to yourself. EFT is a wonderful way to clear the blockages you discover with Kinesiology, so the combination is very powerful.

Once you have encountered a blockage using Kinesiology, you need to decide what to do next. In some cases, the response to the muscle test may trigger new understanding in the receiver that will provide a direction for EFT. In other cases, the recipient may not have any conscious understanding of the response. This is fine, too. All you need to know is the nature of the PR. With the basic levels of PR, you can usually overcome the blockage by changing the standard affirmation to address the specific nature of the reversal and continuing with EFT in the usual way. Figure 5.2 gives examples of affirmations to use with each of the levels of psychological reversal.

TIPS FOR SUCCESS AND ACCURACY

Small changes in technique can produce big changes in the results you get using Kinesiology. As we have mentioned, successful use of Kinesiology generally requires practice. The following suggestions may also help you to increase your effectiveness with kinesiology.

   1. **Use test statements to confirm accuracy.** We discussed this before, but it is so important, it deserves repeating here. Always start with some test statements to be sure the receiver is

---

FIGURE 5.2
AFFIRMATIONS TO OVERCOME THE LEVELS OF PR

LEVEL OF PR	AFFIRMATION TO USE IN THE EFT SEQUENCE
"I want to get over this _____."	"Even though I don't want to get over this _____, I deeply and completely accept myself."
"I want to <u>completely</u> get over this _____."	"Even though I don't want to completely get over this _____, I deeply and completely accept myself."
"I <u>will</u> get over this _____."	"Even though I don't think that I will ever get over this _____, I deeply and completely accept myself."
"I believe that I can get over this _____."	"Even though I don't believe I can get over this _____, I deeply and completely accept myself."
"I deserve to get over this _____."	"Even though I don't believe that I deserve to get over this _____, I deeply and completely accept myself."

responding well. Start with his or her name. Then test other simple statements, like the city you are in, the current year, etc. If you are not able to get accurate responses to these questions, we do not recommend proceeding further with testing.

2. **Be sure the receiver is ready.** Always finish the statement you are testing before applying pressure and be sure the receiver is resisting. Say the statement, like "My name is Joe," and have the receiver repeat it aloud. Then say "resist" just before pushing to be sure the receiver is resisting.

3. **If in doubt, repeat the test.** If there is any doubt about whether the receiver was distracted or whether the result was strong or weak, repeat the test. You can also use the opposite statement, such as "I deserve..." and "I don't deserve..." to confirm the result.

4. **Be sure the receiver is not pushing upward.** The receiver should be resisting the downward pressure, not pushing upward. Pushing upward involves other muscles and will interfere with the accuracy of the results.

5. **Communicate with the receiver.** Issues like deserving to improve or having the ability to improve in an area of a person's life are subtle, but the receiver may know where the problem lies or experience a sudden recognition about the source of the problem. When you get significant test results, ask if the receiver understands what they mean.

6. **Keep the ego out of the way.** Muscle testing is not a contest. Any kind of competitive battle, where the provider and/or the receiver are trying to prove something, will interfere with the results. Being neutral about the results is the keys to successful muscle testing for both the provider and the receiver.

7. **Relax and take your time.** Test responses are sometimes confusing, so it is important not to rush yourself. You may have to stop and think for a moment to be sure that you understand what the result of a test means.

For example, if a person tests strong for "Focus on anger," what does this mean? Whatever a person tests strong for, their unconscious takes as positive or necessary. A strong response to focusing on anger means that the receiver considers anger to be positive or necessary. A balanced reaction to a negative emotion is a weak response, so this person has a problem with anger. It may also take some time to determine how to proceed with EFT once the nature of a blockage has been determined.

The EFT Video mentioned earlier shows how to use Kinesiology with EFT. Refer to Appendix B for more information.

MORE SAMPLE QUESTIONS

There are countless statements that you could test with Kinesiology. Its use can be an enlightening experience in itself, as you explore the realms of your unconscious mind.

We all have goals in life. Here are some statements that relate to achieving these goals:

1. "I want to _____." Examples:

   - "I want to exercise."
   - "I want to be a couch potato."
   - "I want to lose weight."

2. "I want to be successful at (or with) _____." Examples:

   - "I want to be successful at work."
   - "I want to be successful at school."
   - "I want to be successful with my marriage."

3. "I deserve _____." Examples:

- "I deserve abundance."
- "I deserve a supportive relationship."
- "I deserve happiness."

Muscle tests performed while focusing on any subject will show whether it makes the receiver feel strong or weak. To be truly free, we need to reach a point where no one else makes us feel weak and no negative emotion makes us feel strong. Here are some statements to test:

4. "Focus on _____." Examples:

- "Focus on your mother."
- "Focus on your father."
- "Focus on fear."
- "Focus on your job."

These examples are a starting point. Questions may be personalized for each individual and problem encountered. As you develop your skills with Kinesiology, you will probably be amazed by what you discover. It is a powerful addition to the EFT techniques that can help to identify the repressed emotions, beliefs, and judgments that stand between you and your goals in life.

CHAPTER SIX

Other Impediments to EFT

Truth is the only
safe ground to stand upon.

- ELIZABETH CADY STANTON

To complete your toolbox of techniques, there are two more conditions that you may encounter and clear when you use EFT. These are the last things to investigate if you are not having success with the techniques you have already learned: the Short and Complete EFT Sequences, and Kinesiology. As you develop your skills, the addition of these techniques should bring your success rate for dealing with troubling emotions up to around 90 percent or more.

NEUROLOGICAL DISORGANIZATION

In a very small percentage of cases, less than 5 percent, a form of energy blockage, which is known as Neurological Disorganization, thwarts the effectiveness of the EFT tapping sequences. To be successful with EFT, you do not need to understand the nature of this blockage. All you need to know is that you can release it by using another one of Dr. Callahan's discoveries. We recommend using this process, which is called the Collarbone Breathing Exercise, when the techniques you have learned so far are not working. If you are not comfortable using Kinesiology, you can try this technique next if you are getting limited results with both the Short Sequence and the Complete Sequence.

THE COLLARBONE BREATHING EXERCISE

At first glance, this procedure may look a bit tricky. For clarity, we demonstrate it on the video in addition to describing it here. Once you get used to the process, it is fairly simple, taking about two minutes. We recommend taking time to familiarize yourself with it for future reference.

You need to keep your elbows and fingers off of the body during this entire exercise, so we recommend holding your elbows out to the side. The exercise involves performing the following breathing exercises while holding your hands in each of eight positions and tapping continuously on the Gamut Point. Start at the end of an exhale.

1. Breathe normally.
2. Breathe in all the way and hold it for about seven taps.
3. Breathe out halfway and hold it for about seven taps.
4. Breathe out all the way and hold it for about seven taps.
5. Breathe in halfway and hold it for about seven taps.
6. Breathe normally for about seven taps.

The eight positions include holding four positions with the right hand and four with the left. You can start with either hand. We will begin with the right:

1. Place the index and middle fingers of your right hand on your right Collarbone Point. No other parts of the hands or arms should be touching the body. With the same two fingers of your left hand, tap continuously on the Gamut Point of your right hand while you perform the six breathing exercises.

2. Repeat the last step with the fingers of your right hand on your left Collarbone Point.

3. Close your right hand into a fist and place the second finger joints on your right Collarbone Point. With your left hand, tap continuously on the Gamut Point while you perform the breathing exercises.

4. Repeat the last step with the second finger joints of your right hand on your left Collarbone Point.

If you need to review the locations of the points, refer again to the descriptions of the Short and Complete Sequences in Chapter Four. Now you will repeat the first four steps with the fingers and second finger joints of your left hand:

5. Place the index and middle fingers of your left hand on your left Collarbone Point. No other parts of the hands should be touching the body. With the same two fingers of your right hand, tap continuously on the Gamut Point of your left hand while you perform the six breathing exercises.

6. Repeat the last step with the fingers of your left hand on your right Collarbone Point.

7. Close your left hand into a fist and place the second finger

joints on your left Collarbone Point. With your right hand, tap continuously on the Gamut Point while you perform the breathing exercises.

8. Repeat the last step with the second finger joints of your left hand on your right Collarbone Point.

When you finish the Collarbone Breathing Exercise, you may return to the Short or Complete Sequence. If you are still not getting results, the last place to look is at energy toxins.

ENERGY TOXINS

We all know that we live in a toxic environment. For the people who do not respond well to EFT even after eliminating PR and using the Collarbone Breathing Exercise, energy toxins may be the problem. This includes people who do not respond at all, those who respond slowly, and those whose problems return quickly. Energy toxins include toxic substances and negative energies that irritate the energy system.

From our clairvoyant work, we have learned to see when toxicity is interfering with healing and try to eliminate it before attempting any deeper work. Things people eat, drink, breathe or come in contact with are the culprits. EFT is ineffective as long as the irritants are present. This discovery of Dr. Callahan's is the final piece of the puzzle that brings the success of these techniques close to 100 percent when dealing with troubling emotions.

Ways to deal with energy toxins

To test for energy toxins, try the following in the order listed:

1. **Change Your Location.** Something in the immediate envi-

ronment may be causing a problem, like a computer, TV, toxic substances in the carpet or fabrics, fragrances in the room, and so on. Go someplace else and try the tapping techniques again. If EFT works, you know that something in the original location is interfering with your well-being. If you are still not having success, go on to Item 2.

2. **Clean Yourself Thoroughly.** Remove your clothing and take a thorough bath without soap, cleaning all areas of your body and your hair thoroughly. There may be something on your clothing that is effecting you, like dry cleaning fluid or laundry detergent. Something you are using on your body could also cause a problem, like hair spray, shampoo or perfume. Once you are clean, try the tapping techniques again before putting on any clothing. This may be awkward if you are helping another person with EFT, but he or she could go home and clean up, then try the tapping techniques again over the phone. If EFT works, you know that something on your body has been interfering with your well-being. If you are still not having success, go on to Item 3.

3. **Wait a Day or Two.** You may have eaten something that created a toxic condition in your body. If this is the case, the tapping techniques will work once the substance has moved completely through your system. To increase your chances for success, you should be careful with what you eat and drink during this waiting period. Your effectiveness will not change if you continue to consume the toxic substance. In this regard, Craig and Fowlie suggest including as much variety in your diet as possible, as even healthy foods may become toxic when consumed too frequently. Here are some of the foods and substances they find harmful for some people.

- Herbs
- Corn
- Coffee
- Caffeine
- Nicotine
- Perfume

- Wheat
- Refined sugar
- Tea
- Alcohol
- Pepper
- Medications

If EFT is still not producing results after waiting a day or two, try GTT. By reaching a deeper level of awareness, these techniques usually produce results with troubling emotions.

ENERGY TOXINS AND KINESIOLOGY

With the addition of muscle testing, you also have the option of testing for toxins that are present in the environment, in substances you are put on your body, and in foods you eat.

Testing Foods

You can test the effect of any food you ingest with Kinesiology. Let us start by taking an example of how the foods we eat affect our bodies. We have found that most people respond poorly to white sugar. This is not true for everyone, but most people muscle weak with Kinesiology when they are holding a sugar cube. To try this on yourself, you just hold some white sugar next to your stomach and perform a muscle test. The strength or weakness of the muscle shows how eating the sugar affects your body. If you test weak, it means that white sugar is harmful to your physical well-being.

You can, of course, use this test for any food. If you suspect that energy toxins are affecting your results with EFT, you may want to test all of the foods on the list above. To carry our food example a step further, we have also found that you can influence the effect of foods with your intent. You can learn more about this in Appendix A.

Testing Other Substances

You can test the substances you put on your body in a manner similar to that used for foods. Here are some examples:

- Place a bottle of lotion next to your skin and test.

- Place a perfume bottle next to your neck or wrist and test. Place a cosmetic bottle where you apply it and test.

- Place a bottle of shampoo, conditioner, or hair coloring next to your hair and test.

In each case, focus your intent on how the product is influencing you as you perform the test. A product that is in harmony with your well-being will test strong. If your muscle tests weak, the product is harmful in some way. You probably would not want to use a product regularly if it is creating difficulty or producing an allergic reaction.

Testing Environmental Influences

In addition to toxic foods and substances, you may also be under the influence of environmental toxins. Figure 6.1 provides a list of toxins that could have a negative effect on your well-being. A strong response to any of these statements means that they are in harmony with your well-being. A weak response means that they are disharmonious.

If you take the concept that everything is energy, then each of us is composed of an energy field or aura. As individuals, each of us holds a unique energetic signature or frequency that distinguishes us from everyone else. It is by connecting with this energy signature that intuitives and clairvoyants are able to "read" people. A skilled intuitive can find out virtually anything about another person by reading his or her energy field.

We are always interacting energetically with the environment around us. It is most beneficial for us to be in a place that is harmonious with our frequency. Being in a supportive environment is like floating calmly on a river of water that is leading us where we want to go in our lives. The temperature is perfect, and the water gently nurtures us as we move forward. In a disharmonious environment, life is more like trying to swim upstream on a raging river. It may take a lot of effort just to stay even, and if we stop swimming, we may find ourselves being swept away from our goals.

When you are in a disharmonious environment, you can easily become overwhelmed, which may create stress or physical illness. A common culprit is the home or office computer. Jane is a sensitive person and she can feel the energy radiating off of a computer if she is anywhere near one. In a similar way, she can feel the pressure that the concentration of electricity places on us, especially in large cities. Whether we are aware of it or not, we are all being influenced by these subtle energies, along with car emissions, and so on.

You can use a technique that is similar to the sugar test for testing the influence of your home or office computer, television, cellular phone, or anything else in your environment. Let us use a computer as an example. First, test yourself while you stand or sit in an area that is away from your computer and any other large concentrations of energy. As you perform the test, focus your intent on how the environment is affecting you. If the environment is neutral, you should test strong. If you test strong for the base test, sit down in front of the computer

FIGURE 6.1
TOXICITY QUESTIONNAIRE

This is a sample list of statements you can test to determine if energy toxins are affecting you. Start each one with the phrase: "Think about your health and well-being in relation to _____," filling in the blank with the phrases on the list below.

STATEMENT	STRONG	WEAK

"Think about your health and well-being in relation to ...

	STRONG	WEAK
... the foods you eat."	_____	_____.
... the foods you ate today."	_____	_____.
... the water you drink."	_____	_____.
... perfumes in your environment."	_____	_____.
... soaps, shampoos and similar products."	_____	_____.
... your childhood vaccinations."	_____	_____.
... medications or other drugs you are taking."	_____	_____.
... aluminum cookware and foil you use."	_____	_____.
... x-rays you have had."	_____	_____.
... the air you breathe."	_____	_____.
... the materials in your home."	_____	_____.
... the materials in your office."	_____	_____.
... the lights in your office."	_____	_____.
... the emotional environment in your home."	_____	_____.
... the emotional environment in your office."	_____	_____.
... your computer."	_____	_____.
... your TV."	_____	_____.

and test yourself again, focusing your intent on how the computer is influencing you energetically.

A strong response to this test indicates that the computer is not interfering with you energetically. A weak response indicates that you are being weakened energetically. If you test weak, you may wish to invest in one of the many protective devices that are available.

Similarly, if you test weak for any of the items in Figure 6.1, you may want to make whatever changes are needed to support your health and well-being.

PREPARE FOR THE UNKNOWN

With the elimination of energy toxins, your exploration of the Emotional Freedom Techniques is complete. You should be able to release almost any type of disturbing emotion you might encounter.

Nonetheless, there is still more for us to explore. With the Getting Thru Techniques (GTT), we are preparing to move into the unknown – into the hidden recesses and vast resources of the unconscious mind. If you have started using Kinesiology, you have probably seen that there is a lot that we do not know about ourselves. Part 3 of this book will help you to develop a direct relationship with your unconscious. This will allow you to understand yourself at a deeper level, and bring more awareness to the changes that occur when you use EFT.

If you are using EFT to deal with physical problems, GTT may be particularly helpful. Repressed emotions often show up in the physical body. With GTT, you can uncover these types of emotions. Once exposed, releasing the emotions with EFT may become the key to improving or completely eliminating a physical problem.

Part 3

GOING DEEPER WITH THE GETTING THRU TECHNIQUES

CHAPTER SEVEN

Getting Thru Holistically

*Your task is not to seek for love,
but merely to seek and find
all the barriers within yourself
that you have built against it.*

- A COURSE IN MIRACLES

The Getting Thru Techniques (GTT) reach into the heart of holistic healing. These processes can help you to bring greater awareness to what is happening in the recesses of your unconscious mind and to integrate the changes that occur as you eliminate your problems.

To achieve true healing, you first need to know what it means to be healthy. Is it just a matter of passing your yearly physical exam? Most people would agree that it is more than that. In addition to having a healthy body, true healing must include having healthy emotions, positive beliefs and attitudes, and a loving relationship with yourself and the world around you. Together, these levels of healing create a sense of balance and wholeness, which are the true signs of health.

Unfortunately, our health system is not yet geared toward wholeness. In the technological age, the human organism has become compartmentalized. Doctors deal with our physical problems. Psychologists address our emotional and mental problems. And spiritual advisors address our religious concerns. For the most part, these professionals prefer not to mix with each other, even though these parts of ourselves are clearly connected in the many ways that we have experienced using EFT. Our next step as a society is to bring them back together and focus on holistic healing.

This chapter explores the Holistic Process, which shows how any problem you are dealing with is connected at the PEM&S levels. Through focused awareness, this process helps you to identify the emotions that are connected with a physical condition and to understand how any problem you are facing is creating limitations in your life. It includes using EFT to release the blockages you encounter, so it builds on the techniques you already know.

THE RETURN TO WHOLENESS

In Chapter One, we described healing as the return to balance and wholeness. When we are this state, there is no conflict. We are free to attract the love, joy, and freedom we have set as the goal throughout this book. Blockages and fragmentation develop when we lose that sense of wholeness.

If the concept of wholeness seems too abstract, you could call it "okayness." In areas of our lives where we are in balance, things are okay. We feel fine about ourselves, things seem to work well, and we feel emotionally positive. Where we are not in balance, things are not okay. We are critical of others and ourselves, things don't seem to work out, and we have troubling emotions. We may even have corresponding physical problems. As we already mentioned, this generally happens as the result of difficult or traumatic experiences, and the influences of authority figures. Most people are okay in some areas and not okay in others.

To understand holistic healing, we need to start with the loss of wholeness. Energetic imbalance starts at the outside of the aura and works its way through all of the levels until it reaches the physical body. Refer again to Figure 2.1, "The Four Levels of Healing."

In the process, the love that exists at the spiritual level is replaced by judgment. We no longer recognize ourselves as being okay. Instead, we judge ourselves as being inherently bad, flawed, or inadequate. Most of us are unaware of these feelings, because we bury them in the unconscious mind.

In this regard, judging others is actually the same as judging ourselves. We may hide our own feelings of inadequacy from ourselves by projecting them onto those around us. Even though it may be hard to admit, most of us have these feelings. We need to love and respect each other along with ourselves to move toward wholeness.

The highest level of healing transforms judgment into love. This is where we find balance and wholeness.

If we are not able to integrate our feelings of inadequacy back to wholeness, the imbalance moves inward to the mental level. Here the judgments limit our freedom through the development of limiting beliefs and attitudes about our abilities to achieve our goals. Instead of understanding that we are free to create what we truly desire, we believe that many things are impossible. Beliefs like "Life is difficult" or "I'll never amount to anything" are externalizations of the judgments we hold about ourselves. As with the judgments, most of our limiting beliefs are hidden in the unconscious mind.

As if this wasn't bad enough, the imbalance then moves to the emotional level, where joy is replaced with fear and other unresolved emotions. Finally it reaches the etheric (energetic physical) level, which is where the meridian system is located. This connects with the physical body, where we experience physical sensations and insecurity. When judgments, limiting beliefs, and painful emotions replace our sense of wholeness, there is generally some level of physical discomfort. We also lose our sense of feeling secure in the world, so we are unable to feel comfortable. We want to escape. Over time, the blockages in the levels of the aura may also reflect themselves in disease or illness.

Every problem you face has corresponding blockages in each of the energetic levels and in the meridian system. This is true whether you suffer from back pain or other physical symptoms, fear or other painful emotions, limiting beliefs, or just feel bad about yourself. To clear the blockages, you need to clear the imbalances from the inside out. You start with the physical level, if you are experiencing something in the body, or the emotional level. From there, you progress to the mental level and finally the spiritual level. This approach allows the blockage to release in an organic way, like peeling the layers of an onion. You start with what you can perceive, which is usually something physical or emotional. Focusing on them allows you to expose what is underneath in your unconscious mind.

The ultimate goal is healing the spiritual level. When this level is clear, all of the levels below it will be clear as well. From this, we can see why physical healing alone is incomplete. It does not clear the blockages at the EM&S levels, so the problem can easily recur.

When you can overcome troubling emotions with EFT, the healing may be complete. The beliefs and judgments often release along with the emotions or through the treatment of PR. If you are still experiencing problems, you may want to try GTT. In this chapter, you will learn to clear all four levels with the Holistic Process. Here is an example of how it works.

JANE'S PROCESS: SORE THROAT

Jane had been troubled with a sore throat for several weeks. Using EFT on the physical symptoms was not helping. She decided to use the Holistic Process to get to the source of the problem and, hopefully, relief from the discomfort. She started her healing process on the physical level by bringing her attention to the soreness in her throat. As she focused on the soreness, she began to feel anger and recalled that she had had a disagreement with an old friend right around the time her throat started hurting. Her friend was becoming increasingly demanding, and was not being considerate of Jane's boundaries. It finally reached the point where Jane could not tolerate it any more, so she told her friend that she was no longer willing to meet the demands.

They had not spoken since, and Jane thought that the friendship might be over. Her anger came from her inability to make the other woman understand her point of view. As she focused on the anger, she also felt sadness that the friendship seemed to be coming to an end. When she focused on the sadness, she felt fear of being lonely without her old friend.

Jane was surprised to realize that she had repressed all of these emotions, but this is common. When we feel unable to work through our emotions, we bury them away in the unconscious where we no longer have to deal with them. This emotional repression frequently leads to physical problems. In Jane's case, it seemed logical that it would show up in her throat, because problems in the throat area are often related to our expression. When we cannot find a way to express ourselves, we may experience the sense of being choked up, or, in this case, having a sore throat.

Once Jane exposed the emotions, she was well on the way to healing. Next she moved to the mental level, by focusing on what was behind the fear. Here Jane recognized that she thought that the world is a tough place to be without friends. She also thought she might not be able to find another friend like the one she felt she had lost. Having uncovered the limiting beliefs, she was ready to move to the spiritual level.

By focusing on how she felt about herself in relation to this situation, Jane realized that she felt like a failure, like she should have been able to make the friendship work out somehow. At the same time, she knew that she had done more than she should have by trying to meet the unreasonable demands her friend was making. She could see now that having a friendship on that basis was not worthwhile.

Having defined all four levels, Jane moved on to clearing with EFT. She started with the anger, because it was the strongest emotion, with an eight on her intensity scale. After one round, it was down to a two. She was feeling much better already. Since the anger was almost gone now, she did the Floor-to-Ceiling Eye Roll, which brought it all the way down to zero. She checked again on the sadness and fear and found that they were gone, too.

When she was finished using EFT, Jane re-evaluated each of the levels. Physically, she noticed that the soreness in her throat was practically gone. Emotionally, she felt relieved, like a weight had been lifted from her. Mentally, she recognized that she could be happy even if she was alone, and that standing by her convictions made her a stronger person. Moving up to the spiritual level, she knew that she would be fine. She was okay. She could feel a lightness in her heart that she had not noticed before. She knew that the process complete.

Feelings in the heart are significant, because this is where we experience the deepest sense of ourselves.

Common phrases like "I know in my heart..." and "My heart tells me..." demonstrate its importance. After completing the process, Jane's sore throat was gone and did not return.

THE HOLISTIC PROCESS

Jane's example shows why this process forms the backbone of our work. Like EFT, you can use it with virtually anything that is wrong in your life. The Holistic Process makes a powerful complement to EFT, because it allows you to reach into your unconscious mind and find out exactly what is happening at the PEM&S levels. With EFT alone, you may miss something, because you do not know that it is there.

Here are some suggestions for using the Holistic Process:

1. **Learn EFT first.** The Holistic Process builds on your EFT skills, so you need to be fluent in the use of EFT before you attempt to do this procedure.

2. **Allow plenty of time.** Reaching into the unconscious to increase your awareness takes more time than EFT. You will be going into a deeper state where you can access information and bring it into full consciousness, so you need to have a block of time available when you will not be interrupted. We generally recommend a minimum of 15 to 30 minutes when you are getting started. With practice, you will eventually be able to access all four levels in a fraction of the time.

3. **Be open and receptive.** Look at yourself honestly and allow whatever is going to be revealed to come forward without judgment. If you feel resistant or afraid of what you might uncover, this is normal. But releasing the limitations you will uncover is the path to true freedom. When you have completed the procedure and cleared the limitations with EFT, you will experience yourself in a new and more profound way.

4. **It may help to approach it like you are looking at someone else.** This is actually true, because the part of you who is experiencing these limitations is not your True Self. The purpose of doing the process is to release the limitations so that you can connect with the truth of who you are.

5. **Familiarize yourself with the Centering Process.** The Holistic Healing also includes the Centering Process in Chapter Five. If you have not done this process yet, practice going through it a few times first. If you are new to guided relaxation methods, this will help you to learn to go into a deeper state of awareness easily. The Centering Process brings you into a neutral and relaxed state where you can explore your inner world.

6. **Learn to bypass the rational mind.** You need to leave your logical, waking mind behind as you reach into the deeper levels of your awareness, where you connect with your intuitive

mind. This happens most easily if you focus fully on each level, and allow any chatter from your rational mind to come and go without drawing your attention. Bypassing the rational mind also allows you to go into a relaxed state.

7. **Focus on your breathing.** If you feel like your focus is waning at any time, just take a couple of deep breaths and focus on how your body feels as you inhale and exhale. The breath has an amazing ability to change your state of mind.

8. **Remember that you are in control.** You can disconnect from an uncomfortable feeling any time you wish. You can also imagine that you are observing it from a distance, like you are 50 or 100 feet away. This may allow you to understand what is happening without feeling uncomfortable.

9. **Practice is the ultimate key to success.** This is particularly true for those who have not done relaxation or guided visualization procedures before. If you experience uncertainty at first, stay with the process, and write down whatever comes into your awareness, whether it makes sense to you or not. The unconscious mind has its own ways of communicating. It may seem foreign at first, so stay with it. As you continue to open to what this deeper part of yourself is trying to tell you, more and more will be revealed. It is like a puzzle that gradually makes more sense as the pieces come together.

You will find a guide for mapping the four levels of the Holistic Process in Figure 7.1. As you go through each one, write down what you discover using this format. This will allow you to pinpoint all of the details. Being in a relaxed state of awareness is much like daydreaming. It is easy to forget things from one moment to the next. This can be inconvenient when you are trying to increase your awareness. To complete

FIGURE 7.1
MAPPING THE FOUR LEVELS OF HEALING

<u>BEFORE</u>

Starting Point (physical condition, emotion or issue).

Write down what is happening on each level before using EFT.

1. **Physical Sensations:** Notice what you feel in your body when you focus on the problem.

2. **Unresolved Emotions:** Focus on the emotions you feel in relation to the problem.

3. **Limiting Beliefs:** Notice how you feel about your possibilities in the world when you focus on the problem.

4. **Judgments:** Notice how you feel about yourself in relation to the problem.

FIGURE 7.1
CONTINUED

AFTER

Write down what is happening on each level after using EFT.

1. **Physical Sensations:** Focus on what you feel now in your body

_____

_____

2. **Unresolved Emotions:** Focus on the emotions you feel now in relation to the problem.

_____

_____

3. **Limiting Beliefs:** Focus on how you feel now about your possibilities in the world.

_____

_____

4. **Judgments:** Focus on how you feel about yourself now.

_____

_____

Summary: How do you feel about the problem after you are done?

_____

_____

_____

the procedure, you will need to recall what you find at each level, so you will want to write down each detail.

Now we will break the process down into steps, as we did with EFT. The five steps are:

1. Identify a Problem
2. Center Yourself
3. Focus on the Levels of Healing
4. Clear the Blockages with EFT
5. Re-Evaluate Each Level

Step 1: Identify A Problem

First you need to decide on an issue to address. You may want to choose a physical condition, an unresolved emotion, or a conflict in your life. If you are not sure what emotions are connected with the problem, you can still use this procedure. All you need to do is to focus on a time when you were troubled by the issue. For example, if your issue is smoking or eating, you need to be able to focus on a time when you wanted a cigarette or some food. Or if your issue is failure, you need to be able to focus on a time when you felt unsuccessful.

If you want to try this process and can't decide where to start, you may want to review the "Feelings Inventory" in Figure 4.3. There are also "Examples of Fears and Phobias" in Figure 7.2. Phobias are simply irrational fears that have no obvious causes. These are some examples of the kinds of concerns that people can overcome using EFT and GTT.

Most of us probably have at least one of these fears or phobias, maybe more. We get so used to them that we tell ourselves "That's just the way I am." It may not even occur to us that it could be different. Well, when you are fluent in the use

FIGURE 7.2
EXAMPLES OF FEARS AND PHOBIAS

- Crowds
- Driving a car
- Flying
- Being alone
- Heights
- Men
- Relaxing
- Foreigners
- Being touched
- Disorder
- Mirrors
- Books
- Being naked
- Motion
- Slimy substances
- Fog
- Enclosed spaces
- Failure
- Cats, dogs, spiders, birds, or other living creatures

- Meeting new people
- Dentists or doctors
- Punishment
- Failure
- Public Speaking
- Women
- Insects
- Criticism
- Rejection
- Imperfection
- Loud noises
- Being dirty
- Rain
- Churches
- Strangers
- Going to bed
- Illness
- Authority figures, like teachers, ministers, the IRS or the police

of EFT and GTT, you no longer have to put up with the fears, phobias, and other painful emotions that prevent you from leading a full life.

Step Two: Center Yourself

Now use the Centering Process in Chapter Five. This will take you into a relaxed state where you can access more information about yourself. If the division between the conscious and unconscious minds is like a brick wall in your normal waking state, it is like a transparent veil when you are in a relaxed, receptive state. Some information is easier to access, and as you develop an ongoing relationship with your unconscious, the entire wall will become more transparent. We have found that after experiencing this state of awareness over time, we could access information from the unconscious with relative ease.

When you finish the Centering Process, make a note of how your body feels physically and how you feel emotionally. Your observations will provide base data to use as you go through the procedure.

Step 3: Focus on the Levels of Healing

When you feel centered and relaxed, you are ready to access information about each of the levels. We recommend that you close your eyes as you focus on each level, then open them, and write down what you have discovered. As we mentioned earlier, you will start at the physical level and work your way out.

1. **Physical Level:** Close your eyes and focus on the problem you want to address. The problem becomes what is commonly known as a doorway, meaning that focusing on it opens the door to the deeper levels of your aware-

ness. You can start with a physical condition, a specific emotion, or some type of issue:

- **A Physical Condition:** If you are experiencing pain or discomfort related to a physical condition, take a deep breath and focus on the area of your body where you are experiencing the discomfort. If you have a physical condition but there is no pain now, just focus on the condition and allow yourself to feel it in a more subtle way. Allow your attention to go to the place(s) in your body where the condition exists and focus on that area. If you do not notice any physical sensations, that is fine; if you do, write them down under "Physical Level."

- **An Emotion:** If you are starting with an emotion, it may be affecting you physically. Sometimes there are obvious connections, like tension headaches. Other times there may be more subtle sensations, pressure, or tension in the body that normally go by unnoticed. Start by closing your eyes, taking a deep breath, and focusing your attention on the emotion. Allow yourself to feel it and notice if there are any sensations in your body that are connected with it. If you do not notice anything, that is fine; if you do, write it down under "Physical Level."

- **Any Other Kind of Issue:** If you are starting with an issue and are not aware of what specific sensations or emotions are connected with it, focus on a time when you experienced the problem. If it relates to a substance like tobacco or food, think of a time when you wanted a cigarette or a time when you wanted food when you were not really hungry. If it relates to something else, such as not being successful or being unwanted, allow all of your attention to go to a time when you felt unsuccessful or unwanted. Allow your body to feel the way it felt then. Take a deep breath and allow your attention to go to the place in your body where there are sensations connected with the issue. Notice how your body feels now compared with how it felt a moment ago when you completed the Centering Process. If you do not notice anything, that is fine; if you do, write it down under "Physical Level."

2. **Emotional Level:** When you have finished with the physical level, you are ready to focus on the emotional level. Start wherever you left off on the physical level. Close your eyes and focus on any sensations you felt. Ask yourself what emotion is behind the sensations. If you are focusing on an issue and did not experience any physical sensations, stay with the issue and ask yourself what emotion is behind the issue.

When an emotion comes into your awareness, allow yourself to feel it without trying to evaluate it. Just breathe energy into it while asking yourself if there are any other emotions behind this one. Sometimes another emotion will come into your awareness. Repeat this procedure until you feel like you have reached the deepest emotion, which is often a form of fear. As you uncover each emotion, write it down in your journal under "Emotional Level."

3. **Mental Level:** With awareness of the deepest emotion, you are ready to move to the mental level. Focus again on the emotion, close your eyes and ask yourself how it makes you feel about your possibilities in the world. You are looking for the limiting beliefs about what you can and cannot accomplish. Each emotional problem has a corresponding belief or beliefs. As they come into your awareness, write each one down under "Mental Level."

If identifying limiting beliefs is a new experience for you, this list of common beliefs may give you a starting point.

- "I will never amount to anything."
- "Life is difficult."
- "Life is unfair."
- "I am responsible for all of my family's problems."
- "I will never be able to keep up with the class."
- "I don't deserve to have the good things in life."
- "No pain, no gain."
- "Nothing comes easily in life."
- "I will never be as successful as a man."
- "Money is evil."
- "I will never be attractive."

You may be wondering how this relates to beliefs like "I am invincible" and "I can do anything." When they are associated with unresolved emotions, they are still limiting. People who put a lot of energy into convincing themselves and others that they are invincible are masking limiting beliefs that they are unable to deal with consciously. If they are honest with themselves, they will find beliefs like "I am vulnerable" and "I feel out of control" behind the invincibility.

4. **Spiritual Level:** Once you have uncovered the limiting beliefs, you are ready to look at how they relate to your concept of yourself. Look over the list of beliefs you have written down, then close your eyes and ask yourself how these limitations make you feel about yourself as a person. Now you are looking for the judgments, which are at the core of any problem. The judgments take us out of a state where we can experience love and wholeness. As they come into your awareness,

write them down in your journal under "Spiritual Level."

If focusing on judgments is a new experience for you, here are some examples:

- "I am inadequate."
- "I am worthless."
- "I am a bad person."
- "I am evil."
- "I am not as good as everyone else."

When you have completed all four levels, you will probably know more about yourself than you did before. After using this process for many years, we are still amazed at the things we discover about ourselves.

If you are having a hard time accepting what you have learned, remember that if you just shove it back down below the surface, it will stay there and continue to create problems in your life. If you are able to release the blockages, you can move toward freedom and wholeness.

Step 4: Clear the Blockages with EFT

With EFT and its affirmations, you can systematically eliminate the unresolved emotions, limiting beliefs, and judgments you have just uncovered. Start with the deepest emotion and the Short Sequence. When you do the affirmation, customize it to address the limiting beliefs and judgments you found at the mental and spiritual levels. If there was more than one emotion, you can continue to use EFT with each one until they are all gone. You may find that after completing just one or two, they will all disappear.

Step 5: Re-Evaluate Each Level

When you have finished releasing the emotions with EFT, you are ready for a review. Take a few deep breaths to return to a centered state. Then focus again on each level:

1. **Physical Level:** Review what you wrote about the physical sensations the first time around. Close your eyes and notice if you feel differently now. In most cases, the physical sensations will diminish or disappear completely along with the emotions. Make note of what you feel in your journal under "Physical Level." In the case of chronic physical conditions, you may want to repeat this procedure on a regular basis over an extended period of time.

2. **Emotional Level:** Review what you wrote about the emotions. Close your eyes and notice how you feel now. If you were able to bring the emotions down to zero with EFT, you should feel noticeably different. Make note of what you feel in your journal under "Emotional Level."

3. **Mental Level:** Review what you wrote about the beliefs. Close your eyes and notice what you believe now. If you were able to bring the emotions down to zero, the beliefs will probably be different, too. Make note of what you believe now in your journal under "Mental Level."

4. **Spiritual Level:** Last but not least, review what you wrote about the judgments. Close your eyes and notice how you feel about yourself now. If the emotions and limiting beliefs have been completely released, you will probably experience yourself in a different way. Take your time here. This is where you can open to the experience of balance and wholeness. As you

do, notice how your sense of self has expanded. Write down how you feel about yourself now under "Spiritual Level."

As with using the EFT techniques alone, this process may be complete in one sitting. As you review each level, you may find that the problem is gone completely or that there is more to explore. If the issue is more complex, with many aspects, you may have to return to it over time. As we mentioned before, this is also true with many physical conditions.

The Holistic Process may look familiar to those who have read Phillip's book, *Getting Thru To Kids*. The five-step process presented there was a version of this one that you can use with children. You can, of course, use EFT with children, too.

THE HOLISTIC PROCESS IN ACTION

We have used the Holistic Process for the last decade with tremendous success. The addition of EFT has made it even more effective. When EFT alone is not providing complete relief from a problem, you can see why this profound process is the next step.

For physical problems, Gary Craig has also reported increased success when dealing with the emotions behind the physical issues. In his e-mail forum, he described a woman who had experienced tremendous pain from fibromyalgia for nearly a decade. When she found out about EFT, she tried using it over a period of a few weeks to relieve the pain. Her results were limited to one or two hours of relief. By accessing the emotions connected with the pain, Gary helped her to clear the source of the pain. As she worked on these issues, her pain subsided to the point where she reported being pain free, except for a little stiffness, which she just tapped away with EFT.

The Holistic Process is equally effective with emotions and

other issues where EFT alone is not working. Sometimes you may not know where to start, like if you are unable to lose weight or have the success you want in your career. This process will provide more information so you can locate the source of the problem. It can take any problem you are experiencing from abstract to concrete.

SAM'S PROCESS: SELF-EXPRESSION

Here is another example of the Holistic Process in action. This time we will follow it step-by-step.

Step 1: Identify a Problem

One of Phillip's clients, whom we will call Sam, had an issue about sharing his viewpoint. He was part of a religious organization that provided inspiration and a community of friends. At the same time, he felt that because of the dictates of the organization, he couldn't express his true feelings at their meetings. This was creating conflict in his life.

Step 2: Center Yourself

Phillip started by leading Sam through the Centering Process. After completing it, he felt relaxed and centered.

Step 3: Focus on the Levels of Healing

Next, they went through the four levels to help Sam understand the situation more clearly. Sam started with the experience of not being able to share his point-of-view.

- **Physical Level:** Sam focused on not expressing himself at the meetings, and Phillip asked him where he felt it in his body. Sam noticed a constriction in his throat and stomach.

- **Emotional Level**: To move to the next level, Phillip asked Sam to take a few deep breaths and focus on how the constriction made him feel emotionally. Sam noticed fear of expressing what he wanted to say. Exploring it further, he felt that fear was the only emotion.

- **Mental Level**: With Phillip's guidance, Sam turned his attention to the thoughts associated with the fear. In examining his possibilities in the situation, he returned to his original dilemma: that he was unable to share his point-of-view. He now saw more clearly how this limiting belief disempowered him.

- **Spiritual Level**: After revealing the self-defeating belief, Phillip asked Sam how this made him feel about himself. Sam struggled with this level. He wanted to go on and correct the limiting belief without recognizing how he was judging himself. After staying with the momentary discomfort, Sam realized that this issue made him feel contracted and small, like he had little value. With this new awareness, he was free to release the judgment he held about himself.

Step 4: Clear the Blockages with EFT

When they started with EFT, Sam estimated the fear to be around a four. One round of the Short Sequence brought the fear down close to zero, but Sam knew that there was another aspect to consider. He felt a deeper level of fear of becoming impatient when expressing his opinions. The impatience was at a six. After another round, the new fear was around a two. The Floor-to-Ceiling Eye Roll brought it close to zero. No more emotions surfaced, so they went on to the next step.

Step Five: Re-Evaluate Each Level

- **Physical Level:** Sam's solar plexus and throat felt much better. There was still a tinge of the constriction, but Sam felt he was still releasing.

- **Emotional Level:** The fear had largely been replaced by joy.

- **Mental Level:** He felt confident that he could express his truth to the group in a harmonious way.

- **Spiritual Level:** Sam felt peaceful, and an image of a serene lake came to his mind. He could picture himself speaking to the group, expressing what he wanted with patience and conviction. He also said he could speak or not speak as needed.

The depth and precision of the Holistic Process amazed Sam. He mentioned afterward that he was surprised at the distinct levels and at how easily each one shifted, taking him into a state of balance and wholeness. He also felt much more aware of himself, empowered to express himself with ease.

When you uncover all four levels of any problem, you learn more about yourself and integrate the changes you experience in a more profound way. This expanded awareness helps you to move forward more consciously on your journey. Your expanded awareness can also help you to relate the problems that those around you are going through with more compassion.

CHAPTER EIGHT
Getting Thru to Your Many Selves

*The psychic realization or discovery of the soul
is not then the end for the seeker,
it is only the very beginning of another voyage
which is made in consciousness
instead of in ignorance.*

- SRI AUROBINDO

The great mystery of the unconscious mind is that it is partly or completely beyond our awareness. We may sincerely believe that we are free of limitation, but below the surface of our awareness, the picture is different. We caught a glimpse of this with the Holistic Process.

We continuously experience this phenomenon in our consultation work and in our own journeys. With our ability to see and feel blockages in the energy field, we can often identify the nature and source of problems people are experiencing and the lessons they need to address. The clients may be completely unaware of these blockages at first, but as they reach into a deeper level of awareness, they, too, can understand what is occurring. They can then clear the blockages and move forward in their lives.

USING IMAGERY

Jane often sees symbolic images that help her to understand where a client is experiencing difficulties. One time she saw an image of a client with bees flying around his head. He was overly occupied with his work, so he was becoming confused and irritable. To achieve balance, he needed to let go of this preoccupation.

Letting go of these kinds of concerns can be difficult, because many of us are diligent and want to do a good job, even when we become overloaded. A similar situation showed up as the image of a ball and chain tied around another client's ankle. In these types of situations, it may be difficult to know what to do, because the imbalance cuts us off from our sense of who we really are, thereby limiting our resourcefulness.

The next Getting Thru Technique, which we call the Unification Process, adds the use of imagery. As we have all seen in our dreams, images are the language of the unconscious. Working with them adds tremendous depth to the healing experience, as it helps us to understand ourselves in a more profound way.

The Unification Process will allow you to see yourself symbolically as you are, from a higher perspective. Adding this elevated level of awareness can help you make amazing changes and understand your true purpose in life. As this process will continue to build on the skills you have already learned, you need to be comfortable doing the Holistic Process before attempting the techniques in this chapter. If you are new to guided visualizations, you can also refer to Figure 8.1 for some keys to success.

YOUR IDEAL SELVES AND SUBPERSONALITIES

In discussing Holistic Healing and the Getting Thru Techniques, we have connected with four levels of our multi-dimensional awareness, PEM&S. The fifth level involves your expression and contains the templates for your Ideal Selves, which could be understood as aspects of the True Self or Soul. Where you are having difficulty, a part of you has disconnected from this ideal, and has come to reflect distortions in the PEM&S levels.

With The Holistic Process, you saw how related emotions, beliefs, and judgments group together around a specific issue. On the fifth level, each group represents a fragmented part of the Soul, which we call a subpersonality or simply a part. Everyone has a number of these subpersonalities who have been cut off from the wholeness of our being and the wisdom of the Soul. Each part corresponds to an issue that we have not been able to integrate. Going back to the tree metaphor from Chapter Four, each grove of trees represents a subpersonality.

Different parts of ourselves surface at different times, depending on the circumstances we are in. One part may surface in social situations, another at work, and yet another when we are under stress. This is the reason why we sometimes become disoriented when we see people out of context. If you run into a person from work when you are at the mall with a friend, you may become uncomfortable. This is because the part of you who hangs around with your friends is not the same one who goes to work the next day. The goal is to integrate all of the

FIGURE 8.1
KEYS TO SUCCESS WITH GUIDED VISUALIZATION

1. **Allow plenty of time:** You cannot rush the exploration of the unconscious mind. Prioritize your time, so you can explore the deeper parts of yourself.

2. **Create a relaxing environment:** You are going into an expanded state of awareness that you access as you relax your body and rational mind. Soft music, candlelight, or a soft cozy comforter can help you to slip more easily into this expanded state.

3. **Set aside the rational mind:** In our normal state, our awareness is generally focused on the rational and logical mind, the left brain. This part of the mind insists on scientific proof and validation through the five normal senses. It has its place, but you need to access deeper levels of your awareness by asking it to wait and evaluate the experience after you are done.

4. **Access the creative mind:** The part of you that can visualize is the right brain, which is the receptive, intuitive part of the mind. You access the creative mind by relaxing and being receptive to whatever unfolds as you focus on a subject you want to explore.

5. **Open to your inner senses:** As your mind relaxes, shift your focus to your body and your breathing, opening to your inner sight, feeling, and hearing. The deepest and most complete experience is a combination of all of the senses. With practice, you will learn how your unconscious mind communicates. It may not be what you expect, so just be open to the experience.

6. **Allow the process to unfold:** When an image enters your awareness, you may not understand what it means right away. Information coming from the unconscious gradually unfolds, much the way a photograph develops in a solution. The rational mind may want to step in and reject it, so the key is to continue to focus on the image. Understanding will follow.

fragmented parts into the wholeness of the Soul.

With each issue, there is an acknowledged part and a dis-owned part that is repressed in the unconscious mind. The ac-knowledged parts represent how we want to present ourselves to the world. Take the example of a person we will call Walter, who wants his friends and family to think he is a nice person. This is the image that an acknowledged part of him wants to project, so he is probably nice to his friends. For another per-son, being nice may not be important. She may prefer to be re-spected. Both are fine qualities, if they come from the wisdom of the Soul.

If, on the other hand, the desire to be nice or respected is related to an unresolved issue, there is another side to the coin. In Walter's case, there may be a disowned part who is still an-gry, because his father disciplined him severely. On the mental level, he felt unable to control the events in his life. On the spiritual level, his experiences left him feeling inadequate. To-gether, the unresolved emotion, limiting belief, and judgment comprise an angry subpersonality who is still unconsciously influencing his life.

Returning to the conscious level, Walter wants to treat those around him better than he was treated as a child, so he tries to be nice. He succeeds most of the time, but now he has to deal with the challenges of having a family of his own. There are stressful times when the repressed angry part comes through, and he hits his children. As is generally true in such cases, Walter quickly represses the anger and vows that he will not ever hit them again. He returns to his image of himself as a nice guy. But regardless of how hard he tries, or how good his intentions are, the problem will not go away until Walter can reconnect consciously with the repressed anger and feelings of inadequacy, so that he can release them once and for all.

This example shows how easily we can be disconnected from powerful unconscious forces that control our lives. Most of us feel like unified whole, and, in a sense, we are. We manage relatively well in most situations, but the disowned parts have a strong influence on our lives. In extreme cases, the subpersonalities are like completely separate people. This condition is known as Multiple Personality Disorder (MPD). People with this condition have generally suffered from severe trauma that resulted in the fragmentation of the Soul into what the individual experiences as different people.

In his book *Peace, Love and Healing*, Dr. Bernie Siegel describes how people with MPD can even change physical characteristics when they change from one personality to another:

> There are certain physiological traits that we assume to be fixed, like diabetes, left- or right-handedness, allergies or color blindness. It appears, however, that people with MPD may be allergic to cats or orange juice in one personality but not in another, may exhibit bums in one personality but not another, may show drug sensitivities in one personality but not another, may switch from being right-handed to being left-handed. I knew someone who had to keep half a dozen different pairs of glasses in her bedside stand, because she didn't know who she would be when she woke up.

The idea that physiological characteristics like allergies and even eyesight may be personality traits is thought provoking. It also shows us that these physical conditions may be altered.

The same is true for the characteristics of your own subpersonalities. Different parts of you may control your finances, your weight, your marriage or primary relationship, your spirituality, and so on. You can learn to reconnect with these fragmented parts with the Unification Process.

Subpersonalities are as varied and unique as individuals. Here are some examples we have encountered:

- One of our clients saw an angry part of himself as a man in a dark suit of armor. The armor was protecting him from being hurt. Unfortunately, his angry expressions were hurting others. This kind of armor is usually protecting the heart, where we feel most vulnerable. The heart is also where we experience judgment of others and ourselves. This man needed to release the judgments he was holding toward himself, so that he could open to more love in his life.

- Another client saw the feminine part of herself as a weak and pale little lady in a white dress. She was so weak that she could barely stand up, and lacked adequate strength to get by in the world. She felt that she had fewer opportunities in life than men have. The lesson for this woman was to embrace her true feminine power, so that she could experience the strength of womanhood and create what she desired in life.

- One of our students who was unable to lose weight saw the part of her who craved food as a drooling monster. The monster was outraged at having been abused as a child, and had built up some strong defenses. She could see that the weight she was holding was protecting her from further abuse and that she needed to release the pain from her past to move forward.

- A client who was experiencing feelings of inadequacy in her business dealings saw herself as a timid little girl in a frilly dress. This little girl was what many would call a wounded inner child, a part of her who was split off in childhood. It is common to encounter childhood aspects of ourselves as we move toward wholeness. Each one is waiting to be understood and integrated back into the whole.

- One time Phillip twisted his ankle while playing basketball. He saw this part of himself as a ghost. He was trying so hard to play well that he had completely forgotten why he wanted to play in the first place. His feet were not even touching the ground, so he was easily thrown off balance and injured. He recognized that he was overcompensating for a lack of confidence and needed to clear the blockages so that he could really enjoy the game.

In revealing these wounded parts of ourselves, the unconscious mind is expressing itself through symbolic images. Each part has a unique story to tell. Some of our examples may seem comical, but they are in earnest. These troubled parts need to be treated with love and respect. Each one has something he or she wants to express, and an issue that needs resolution to return to wholeness.

The value of understanding and reconnecting with your Ideal Self is that this part of you already has the solutions to your problems. People sometimes refer to this Ideal Self as their creative intelligence or super intelligence. It is the part of you that can point the way to freedom. Refer to Figure 8.2 for an illustration of how the fragmented subpersonalities are cut off from the light of the Soul. This figure also illustrates shows how the spiritual journey unfolds, as you integrate the disowned parts of yourself into the unity of the soul.

The Ideal Selves also have unique characteristics, which are generally inspirational. Here are some examples:

- For any physical problem, you have your own Inner Healer. This part may look like a doctor in a clean white coat with a stethoscope hanging around his neck or a wise woman who has advice on the deeper nature of healing.

- For weight, you can connect with your Ideal Body. For a per-

FIGURE 8.2
UNIFYING THE FRAGMENTED SUBPERSONALITIES

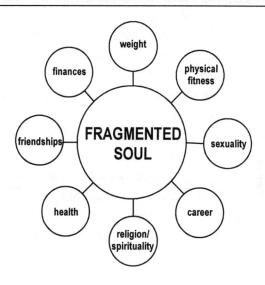

son with a weight problem, this part is already at their ideal weight, looking wonderful. This part usually feels energetic and confident.

For spiritual issues, you may encounter an angel or a wise sage with profound wisdom to share. This enlightened being can provide assistance with any kind of decision you need to make, and bring more understanding to any problem you face.

In each case, these Ideal Selves connect you with resources and wisdom you never knew you had. By allowing yourself to focus on what they have to share, you can experience a profound level of awareness. You can also focus on them throughout the day to help bring this ideal into your life. They can bring healing, help you to move toward your ideal weight, and much more. You will have an opportunity to experience this for yourself with the Unification Process.

THE UNIFICATION PROCESS

The Unification Process can bring greater understanding to any problem. It allows you to connect with a fragmented part of yourself and re-unify him or her with the Ideal Self.

To begin, you need to find a quiet, comfortable place where you can relax undisturbed. If you have practiced the other processes in this book, you should be able to read this one and close your eyes at intervals to connect with yourself and allow the images to unfold. You can also take a few deep breaths at any time to deepen the experience. Have your journal handy to write down the information you receive. This will help you to focus and to recall the details of your experience later.

Before you start, it is important to decide on a single issue to address. As with EFT, you can only focus on one problem at a time with this procedure.

You are ready to begin. Remember to read the words slowly, allowing them to carry you into a deeper state of awareness.

As you read each word and begin to relax, take a few deep breaths and feel the tension beginning to melt from your body. Fill your lungs completely with pure, clear air with each inhale. Allow the tension to continue to release with each exhale, so that with each breath, you feel more and more relaxed, and your body becomes lighter, allowing the tension to drift down through your arms, legs, and feet, into the earth.

Bring clear energy into your mind with each inhale, so that all of the cells of your brain can relax, and your mind becomes more and more clear with each breath. And allow the clear energy to move down, so that your entire head is relaxed. Feel the energy travelling down past your neck and shoulders now, allowing all of the organs in your body to relax. Now allow a wave of clear energy and relaxation to move gently down your arms, all the way down to the tips of your fingers. And feel another wave of relaxation moving down your body to your legs and feet, reaching all the way to the tips of your toes, so your entire body is relaxed and filled with clear, pure energy.

Notice how relaxed you feel now. From this peaceful place, begin to connect with a part of yourself who has a problem you want to address. It may be the part of you who is stressed, overweight, unhealthy, physically inactive, or who smokes cigarettes.

Before going further, remember that you are in complete control. If what you experience is painful in any way, you can stop at any time. You can also move yourself away from the scene, as if it is 50 feet or even 100 feet away, wherever you feel comfortable. As you connect with yourself in this way, you will see how your unconscious sees you, and as you continue with this process, the image will change.

Now recall a time when you experienced the problem you are focusing on, such as when you were eating for a reason other than hunger, when you felt stressed, when you were in pain, or wanted to smoke a cigarette. You will find the right time. If no time comes to mind, you can just focus on the issue and allow a representative scene to unfold. If you have already done this process with the same issue, you can go back to another time, or repeat the same one and make note of the changes.

Take a couple of deep breaths and recall the scene. Remember that you can close your eyes at any time, take a few more deep breaths and connect with the experience at a deeper level. Allow yourself to feel the emotions you have felt before related to this problem. How do you feel physically? How much energy do you have? How do you feel emotionally? How do you feel about your possibilities in the world? How do you feel about yourself? Take plenty of time to notice each of these levels. You can map all four levels in your journal as you did with the Holistic Process.

Now, focus on visualizing the part of yourself who is experiencing this problem. As you continue to focus on yourself, make note of what you see: the size of your body, the shape, the clothing you are wearing, the expression on your face, the way your hair looks, and so on. Make note of any details you notice about this part of you. If you don't think you see anything, just allow yourself to imagine how this part of you would look if you could see yourself and make note of that.

Also, make note of the scene around you. Notice where you are, if there are other people there, and anything else that draws your attention. The scene may be related to a real event from your past or symbolic of the problem you are experiencing. It may also be a combination of both. Just allow yourself to notice what is there. Now, imagine that if there were any sounds associated with this scene, how would they sound? What volume? How harmonious? What type of rhythm, if any? And if you were to associate a color with this scene, what would it be? See and feel this color around yourself and allow the image to become completely clear in your mind, experiencing it with all of your senses, the feelings in your body, the emotions, how it looks and sounds, even any scents in the air and tastes in your mouth.

As a note, what you are looking for here is the way your unconscious mind relates to the scene, not the way you want it to be. Your mind may want to switch to something else, so you need to keep your focus. You will have an opportunity to change it soon.

When the image is complete, allow yourself to rise above it, so that it is like a photograph or picture on a screen that you can see below you, separate from yourself. Allow yourself to gently drift to a peaceful spot, maybe in some puffy white clouds or on a mountaintop, whatever is right for you. When you arrive, find a comfortable place where you can relax, like a billowy cloud or some soft grass that is perfectly contoured to fit your body.

When you are settled in this relaxing place, you may want to take a few moments to work with the emotions you just experienced with EFT. Review all of the levels you noted in your journal and clear the patterns with EFT as you have done before.

When you have completed the EFT, you are ready to continue, even if you were not able to reduce the intensity of the emotions you were experiencing all the way to zero. Just focus on being in that peaceful place and take some pure, loving breaths. Allow these breaths to send this beautiful energy through your entire body. Notice if there are any places that feel tense, and send energy there, until your whole body is relaxed and filled with pure, loving energy.

As you continue, begin to focus your breath on the area around your heart, which is where your Soul connects with the body. Imagine that you are sending pure energy into this area, so that with each breath, there is more and more energy there. As you continue breathing, you can feel the energy building so there is a ball of light there around your heart. Allow this ball of light to become brighter and brighter, radiating its energy out in all directions, so that you feel yourself completely surrounded by the energy, and you can feel this energy permeate every cell of your body with its beautiful light.

As you do this, if any pain comes up in your heart, simply allow the pain to come out into your awareness, because releasing this pain will help you to completely embrace the love you hold in your heart. If necessary, you can stop and do more EFT to release anything that may come up as you focus on your heart.

Now shift your awareness to the area just above your head and imagine another light there. As you imagine it there, allow this light to begin to pour down through the top of your head and fill your entire body, so that you can see and feel yourself filled with the light all the way down to the tips of your fingers and the tips of your toes. As it becomes brighter and brighter, it overflows so that you are completely surrounded with this light, and you can feel yourself in perfect harmony and balance with everything around you.

In this harmonious state, you can easily contact your Ideal Self, the perfected part of you who is waiting to come into your life. As with the first image, you can focus on the ideal you in relation to your weight, your health, or any problem you are dealing with. Imagine that you are in that state of perfection, and sense how this ideal part of you feels physically. How much energy do you have? How do you feel emotionally? How do you feel about yourself? Now, as you continue to imagine this Ideal Self in your mind, make note of what you see. What is the size of your body, the shape, expression on your face, clothing, hair, and so on. Make note of all the details as you did before.

And again, if you don't think you see anything in your mind's eye, just allow yourself to imagine how you would look ideally, and make note of that. Now, imagine that if there were any sounds associated with this image, what would they be? What volume? How harmonious? What type of rhythm, if any? And if you were to associate a color with this image, what would it be? Surround yourself with the color and experience the entire image with all of your senses. Notice the feelings in your body, the emotions, the sights, and the sounds. Now ask yourself how this ideal part of you feels about the problem you have been dealing with? Spend a little time getting to know this Ideal You. If you want to, you can also use this level of awareness to form strategies to make the changes you desire.

Now, staying in contact with your Ideal Self, look down at the image you created earlier, which you left below you. From this peaceful place, send the color you are now surrounded with down to completely surround the old image. Now follow the color down into that original scene, but bring along all of the feelings, the sights and sounds that you associated with your Ideal Self. Look around and see how the old scene looks to you now. Has it changed? How do you feel about yourself? How much energy and vitality do you have in your body? How do you look? And how do you feel about the problem that was bothering you before?

If this image and your reactions to it have changed from the way they were before, if they are closer to your Ideal Self, you are on the way to making this Ideal You a reality in your life now and, because of this, your future will be different.

And as you strengthen your relationship with this Ideal You, communicate. Allow him or her to share with you all the special and unique qualities you have to contribute.

Now you have an opportunity to look forward in time, to

project the image of your Ideal Self out into your future. Again, feel yourself surrounded by the color of your Ideal Self. Experience all the feelings and, see the image in your mind. Imagine that the past is behind you and the future is laid out in front of you. Send the color of your Ideal Self out into the future, reaching out toward the horizon, completely surrounding all of your future experiences, and extending way out, as far into the future as you can imagine.

Now, imagine yourself moving forward to a time in the future when you would previously have expected to encounter the problem you are focusing on. Again, experience being your Ideal Self with all of your senses. Notice the sights, feelings, and sounds. Do you feel like you have overcome the problem now? If so, just remember that you can contact this perfect part of yourself at any time. Simply breathe loving breaths, and remember the color and image, and bring it all around yourself. Over time, this will help you to move closer and closer to that ideal.

If you were not able to fully experience your Ideal Self in the present or the future, just continue to work with this process, and use EFT on the emotions that come up. You will notice a shift as you move closer and closer to the ideal. Releasing the emotions will bring you closer to experiencing your Ideal Self. Above all, continue to breathe those loving breaths.

Now it is time to shift your awareness back to the present moment, and feel yourself where you are, sitting or lying down, making note of your body's position. And, as you breathe, allow your breath to bring you back to your normal waking state, feeling alert and alive, bringing your Ideal Self with you into your daily life.

This procedure allows you to fully understand and resolve any problem you may encounter. Here is an example.

BRIAN'S PROCESS: BUSINESS SUCCESS

Phillip had a session with a client we will call Brian. Brian was starting a new business and was concerned about his ability to succeed. They went through the Unification Process to find out where the concerns were coming from.

When Brian closed his eyes and focused on these concerns, he saw a 12-year-old version of himself crying. Physically, he noticed heaviness in his heart and tension all over his body. Emotionally the 12-year-old felt disappointment and frustration. Mentally, he uncovered several beliefs. He believed that even if he could try hard, things would never come out the way he wanted anyhow. Because of this, he determined that the world is unfair, so why bother trying to succeed? Moving to the judgments, the young fellow felt weak, unwanted, discredited, and rejected by others.

It is easy to understand how a 12-year-old boy could feel this way. Unfortunately, Brian had carried these feelings into his adulthood, where they were blocking his ability to succeed. Phillip and Brian did some EFT on the frustration. They also addressed his specific beliefs in the affirmation by saying "Even though I have this frustration, I completely accept myself. Even though things never come out the way I want them to, I completely accept myself. Even though the world is unfair, I completely accept myself." Brian's emotional intensity started at around a six and went down in one round to a one or two. After doing the Floor-to-Ceiling Eye Roll, it was gone completely.

Once the emotional charge was reduced, Phillip and Brian took another look at how the boy was doing. The 12-year-old was happy now, and, as Brian focused on the image, he felt the boy merge with him as an adult. This sometimes happens as the fragmented subpersonalities re-integrate. It can be quite a profound experience, and means that the process is complete. Then Brian saw an image of himself as an adult. He knew that he could now deal with his success in a mature way. Physically, he noticed that his body felt relaxed now, and his heart felt light. Emotionally, he felt contented. Hope had replaced his feelings of hopelessness. Mentally, he knew that he could succeed. Spiritually, strength had replaced his feelings of weakness. Brian could now accept himself in a more profound way, and was prepared to move ahead toward his goal.

Phillip made another useful observation about this process. During the entire session, Brian found himself yawning. Phillip understood that the yawning was Brian's way of releasing stuck energy. It allowed Brian to take deep breaths, as the energy reconfigured around him.

When we make a change within ourselves, the entire energy field reconfigures itself to accommodate the new level of awareness. Some people can actually feel this shift happening.

As Phillip and Brian finished, Brian could also tell that he was still in the process of integrating the experience and that he would understand it more clearly in the coming days.

We have one final note about Brian. Before doing this procedure, he was completely unaware of what was occurring in his unconscious mind. He recognized afterwards that he would have had a hard time succeeding in his new business as long as the 12-year-old part of him was in control. He was highly impressed with how quickly and how deeply the process worked.

Another step that can help with integrating change is the Break Thru Process. This technique provides a way to create a brighter future for yourself.

THE BREAK THRU PROCESS

Oprah Winfrey has credited her success in overcoming enormous challenges in her life to making a firm decision to change. From the perspective of the subpersonalities, she is referring to enlisting all of her resources to take her where she wants to go by sending a strong message to the unconscious. Much of the time, part of us wants to change and another equally strong part wants us not to change. With all of these fragmented parts, it's a wonder we can get anything done. The first step in any process that involves making lasting changes is to address the levels of healing and the subpersonalities connected with a problem. Once this groundwork is done, you have to decide that it is time to make the change. This is the purpose of the Break Thru Process. You can use it to literally break through any limitation in your life. You may want to use it on the day when you decide to stop smoking or when you are ready to change any other habit or pattern of behavior.

The Break Thru Process is quite profound.

At any moment, you can decide that things are going to be different from now on and leave your reservations behind.

You can move beyond your limitations and create a positive future for yourself. You can also move beyond a perpetual state of healing, where you continually live in the shadows of your wounded inner child and other conflicts. You can even recover from recovering.

Before attempting this technique, do the Unification Process and connect with your Ideal Self related to the problem. Have a pad of paper or a journal handy to note the details of your experience, to help you focus and for future reference.

Start as before in a quiet, comfortable place where you can relax undisturbed. Remember that you can close your eyes whenever you wish to visualize. You can also take a few deep breaths to go deeper at any time. Begin by reading each word slowly to yourself as you allow yourself to relax.

When you have made yourself comfortable, you can start by taking a few deep breaths and allowing any tension you feel in your body to begin to melt away, completely filling your lungs with pure, clear air and allowing more tension to release with each exhale. With each breath, allow yourself to feel more relaxed and notice your body becoming lighter and lighter. Allow the tension you are releasing to melt down through your body, legs and feet, and into the earth. As you continue to breathe, allow the breath to be loving and nurturing, embracing yourself with relaxation.

Now, feel yourself becoming even lighter with each breath, like you are breathing in extra light air. After a few breaths, you should feel light enough to imagine yourself floating gently up into the sky. Just imagine that you are drifting gently along into a beautiful mist, feeling very light and floating freely.

As you continue drifting, imagine that you are arriving at a peaceful place on the top of a hill where the mist is beginning to clear. Looking around, notice that you are standing on a path, with your past extending behind you and the future extending before you. Directly in front of you is a gate. Look at this gate and make note of its appearance, its color, materials, and any details. Look beyond the gate and see the color of your Ideal Self from the Unification Process permeating your future.

Now prepare to turn around for a moment, and look at the past. As you do this, remember that you are in control of your experience. If there are painful memories, you can keep them at a distance, as you did with the Unification Process. That way, you can review them and move beyond them with ease. You may also disengage yourself from them whenever you choose.

Now as you turn to face the past, allow yourself to bring anything that you need to see or understand about the problem you are dealing with to your awareness. This is an opportunity to observe the details, knowing that you can simply choose to leave them behind when you are ready to move through the gate into your future, because you can break thru at any time. This can be the day when you decide that things will be different from now on, that you will be different. The choice is yours.

As you look back into the past, you may want to look at your childhood or later in life. If you have done this process before, look for something new this time, something you may have missed before, but are ready to see today.

Take a few minutes to really examine your past, as a neutral observer. Take a kind and honest look at how you have related to the problem you are facing. Examine the specific times when it has been most difficult for you. Allow yourself to feel the emotions you have felt before. This may be a good time to allow your thoughts and feelings to come out on paper. And make note of any ways that your relationship to this problem in the past has prevented you from becoming that Ideal You, your True Self.

When you have finished examining your past, it is time to consider moving through the gate into the future, leaving behind any limitations that you are ready to release. You can literally break thru into a new life where anything is possible, where becoming your Ideal Self is a reality. Before you go, however, you can take a few minutes to release any emotions you have brought up from the past with EFT. Take some time for this now. Then you can return to the procedure.

If you don't feel like you are ready to make any changes now, you can wait and go through the gate at another time. In this case, keep repeating this process, and record what you notice about yourself and what prevents you from becoming your ideal.

Now it is almost time to move through the gate. First, turn back toward the past and take a final look at the limitations you are leaving behind. The past may already look different if you did some clearing with EFT. If you haven't written them down, take a moment to write down the limitations you are going to leave behind when you go through the gate. This may be the moment that you leave the limitation of being a smoker, a compulsive eater, or a shy person behind. It is up to you.

Recognize how significant this moment can be. This is the moment when everything can change. As you turn back to face the gate, notice that off to the right, there is a purple flame, a transformational flame where you can throw all of the old patterns of behavior, old beliefs, old emotions, all of the limitations you are ready to discard. Before you go through the gate, take a moment to throw each limitation into the flame, watching it light up as the fire transforms it into an unlimited possibility for the future.

As a note, you can also throw any reservations you have about succeeding with your goal into the flame and clear the reservations with EFT. Take whatever time you need now for EFT.

If there are any other things that are holding you back, toss them in the flame. Now, find the handle or latch on the gate, open it, and look out into the future, seeing the color of your Ideal Self permeating the scene before you. When you are ready, walk through the gate.

Once you are on the other side, make note of how you feel.

Fill yourself with the color of your Ideal Self, feel the sensations and emotions, hear the sounds, notice how your Ideal Self appears, the clothing, all the details. Look around you. Gaze into your future. How do you relate now to the things you explored in your past? Congratulate yourself for the changes you have made. Look out further into your future now. Notice the color of your Ideal Self extending out as far as you can see, and feel yourself starting to move down the path, as you begin to come back to your normal waking state.

Now, become aware of your breath again, and breathe in active energy to make you feel alert and vitally alive as you imagine drifting back through the mist to your seat, feeling your body resting gently, allowing your toes to wiggle a bit, and become totally awake and ready to move on.

A NOTE ON FULFILLMENT

With EFT and GTT, you now have some of the most powerful tools available for making positive changes in your life. Before moving on to relationships in the next chapter, we want to mention one more thing: your perspective. The best place to look to for abundance, freedom, or anything else that represents fulfillment in your life is within yourself. You are already well on the way after reading this far.

Unfortunately, our society does not teach us to seek fulfillment within ourselves. Advertisers want us to believe that more money, an expensive car, a new outfit, the right cigarette or a trip to the Caribbean will solve all of our problems. You can probably see why this emphasis on external rewards is so ineffective. Wherever we go, we take ourselves, our unresolved emotions, limiting beliefs, and judgments. It is within ourselves that we will find key to unlimited joy, love, and freedom.

When you decide that you want to accomplish something in your life, it is important to know what you really expect to achieve. Will a million dollars bring you joy? Will a husband or wife and a new home complete your life, so you can live happily ever after? Will drugs solve your problems?

When you are looking for something outside yourself, what are you really looking for? If a relationship represents financial security, self-esteem, a clean house, or anything else that you need to have to be complete within yourself, examine your own issues first. Then you can create a genuinely fulfilling and supportive relationship.

Money is clearly the biggest attraction in our society. Many people believe that it alone is the key to happiness, security, and stress relief. What does it represent to you? If you expect it to solve all of your problems, as so many lottery enthusiasts do, you are bound to be disappointed. Statistics show that money and fulfillment in life are not necessarily related. To experience genuine fulfillment, you have to deal with your unresolved emotions and issues. Then you can really enjoy your money, your new car, or whatever you choose to have.

As you continue to explore the GTT processes, we recommend making a list in your journal of the material things you want to have and what each one represents to you. As you release the blockages that stand in your way, you will find that your desire for external rewards changes. Interestingly, as you become clearer, more and more abundance will also flow into your life. Then you can really enjoy it.

CHAPTER NINE

Getting Thru to Others

Friendship, like love,
is the most important bread and butter for life.

- ANGNA ENTERS

Our relationships are like the fabric that forms the tapestry of our lives. It is through our interactions with others that we learn about ourselves and share our experiences. Other people are our friends, teachers, companions, and lovers. They give our lives meaning.

Most relationships go through tough times. In addition to enhancing our lives, the people around us trigger emotions like fear, anger and anxiety. For many people these emotions continue to manifest unchecked and create stress. They can place strains on even the best relationships. With EFT and GTT, you can examine the emotions you feel toward others, increase your understanding, and clear your way to freedom.

The saying "It takes two to tango" refers to how people trigger negative responses in one another. You cannot change another person, but you can control how they affect you and influence your life. A lot of our difficulties are just minor irritations that we can easily tap away with EFT. As we clear these unresolved emotions within ourselves, our relationships improve. If you just pick out one such emotion to tap on each day, you will be amazed with the results. You will begin to look at those around you through new eyes.

When we are harboring emotions like resentment, anger, or hostility, people around us can sense the discord below the surface. This is even true when we are keeping our feelings to ourselves; the negative undertone creates a barrier between people. On the other hand, people tend to respond favorably when we are more positive ourselves. Carpooling can become much easier. Those phone calls where you have to listen to recorded messages and wait for five minutes before speaking with an actual person become less irritating. Driving in rush hour traffic may even become a relaxing experience once you eliminate the anger and frustration so many people experience in congested traffic. With EFT, you can choose if you want to experience frustration or peacefulness in any situation.

Some issues are more complex. EFT and GTT may not be enough to salvage an unhealthy relationship. A client we will call Kelly held a lot of hostility toward her father's second wife. Kelly's mother died many years ago. They were a very loving family, and Kelly missed her mother deeply. To make matters worse, her father remarried a very possessive woman. The new wife did not want Kelly's father to see his children, and he complied with her wishes. When Kelly had children of her own, they never had an opportunity to get to know their grandfather. This was so painful for Kelly that she held onto her anger toward her father's new wife nearly twenty years.

Jane understood the pain Kelly felt at losing her father, but Kelly needed to understand that she chose the effect it had on her. By harboring anger, she was only hurting herself. She was miserable, and she was allowing the new wife to control her life. With Jane's help, Kelly released her anger with EFT. She was amazed with the changes she experienced in her life. Her relationship with her father was unchanged, but her family life improved. She realized that she had been taking her unresolved anger out on those around her.

RELATIONSHIPS AND WHOLENESS

When we view life as a journey to wholeness, our relationships take on deeper meaning. They help us to learn about ourselves. We see how different parts of ourselves relate to different parts of others. When we are in a state of balance and wholeness, we are complete. We love and honor others and ourselves. When we lose this balance, judgment, limiting beliefs, and painful emotions replace love and honor. The wisdom of the Soul is replaced by co-dependence.

Co-Dependence

In his book *Co-Dependence: Healing the Human Condition*, Charles Whitfield defines co-dependence as "a disease of lost selfhood." When we are functioning from wholeness, we are self-empowered, relying primarily on the Soul as our guide. We can appreciate other people's contributions and learn from those around us, while maintaining our sense of self-worth.

What often happens is that we give our true power away. Through traumatic experiences and negative programming, we begin to believe that we are somehow defective and inadequate. We value the opinions of others above our own, and rely on others, rather than ourselves, for our sense of self worth. When this occurs, the Soul goes into hiding, replaced by a false co-dependent self or subpersonality.

Co-dependent relationships are polarized. Some people allow others to control their lives; some seek to have control over others. Neither one has genuine empowerment, which honors both parties equally.

From the definition, it is easy to understand that relationship problems are a characteristic of co-dependence. Charles Whitfield estimates that 95 percent of the population is co-dependent, with 25 percent being more severely wounded. Figure 9.1 lists "The Characteristics of Co-Dependence." As with all of our problems, the key to transforming these relationships is clearing the emotions, beliefs and judgments that have fragmented us from the wisdom of the Soul.

Enabling and Boundaries

An important aspect of co-dependence is the tendency to internalize another person's problems and unconsciously contribute to their destructive behavior. When this occurs, a child may relate being wounded to being bad, like it is her fault. "If I am good, then my father won't get drunk and hurt my mother." Or the abused wife: "If I make the right dinner, then my husband will not become angry."

This attempt to "fix" another person's problem is known as enabling and both sides of the relationship are co-dependent. Correcting this problem requires both people to take responsibility for themselves and establish healthy boundaries.

Boundaries represent the divisions we maintain between

FIGURE 9.1
THE CHARACTERISTICS OF CO-DEPENDENCE

QUALITIES	CO-DEPENDENT SELF	BALANCED SELF
Expectations	Expects relationships to fill needs individual unable fill for him- or herself	Expects relationships to enhance experience of life, takes full responsibility for him- or herself
Expression	Fragmented subpersonality, cut off from the Soul	Unified self, connected with the wisdom of the Soul
Balance of Giving and Receiving	Out of balance, either self-defacing, valuing others over self and giving power away or self-absorbed, valuing self over others, takes others' power	In balance, feeling self-empowered, able to love, honor and value self and others equally
Boundaries	Unhealthy, unable to maintain balance between giving and receiving	Healthy, able to maintain balance between giving and receiving
Results	Experience of judgment, limiting beliefs and unresolved emotions	Experience of joy, love and freedom

ourselves and the people we interact with. Healthy boundaries provide a balance between giving and receiving. We need to have healthy boundaries at home, at work, and any other place where we interact with others.

Healthy boundaries allow everyone to meet their needs.

Self-absorbed people tend to take more than they give. Self-defacing people tend to lose sight of their needs by attempting to please others. They may attempt to single-handedly meet the needs of all of the people around them. Setting boundaries is about defining your territory, on all levels: physically, emotionally, mentally, and spiritually. For most of us, this is one of life's largest challenges. We need to be able to let others know what is ours, what we are willing to share, and what type of behavior is appropriate around us.

NEUTRALIZING CONFLICTS WITH OTHERS

We have helped many people with their relationships in our classes and personal consultations. Phillip has also helped his emotionally disturbed students to learn to get along with each other and develop effective social skills. We have found these to be important points to consider with relationships:

1. **Everyone is doing his or her best.** Even hardened criminals believe that they are doing the best they can with the hands they have been dealt. In many cases, people simply do not have adequate resources to deal successfully with the circumstances they find themselves in. Understanding their limitations can help you to have compassion.

2. **You cannot change another person.** The only real work that can be done is to change the way you relate to the other person. As you move toward wholeness within yourself, the way the other person relates to you will probably change too.

3. **Distinguish between the person and his or her behavior.** You can love and honor another person, while disliking specific behavior. Rather than saying "You irritate me," which implies that you are referring to the whole person, you can say "Your tone of voice irritates me" and address the behavior.

4. **Honor each person's uniqueness.** People understand the world in very different ways. We each have a set of fears, goals, rules, belief systems, and ideas of what is important. These differences can create conflict if we expect everyone else to be just like us. To improve relationships, we need to expand our awareness to see the world through other people's eyes. This helps us to understand why people behave the way they do, and allows us to expand our opportunities to learn and grow.

5. **Discuss conflicts when you are in a neutral state.** When you are in the heat of battle, experiencing anger, resentment, or any other negative emotion, your ability to think clearly is impaired. You are functioning from a fragmented part of yourself who is disconnected from the wisdom of your Soul.

To resolve conflicts effectively, you need to be in a clear state of mind where you can express your feelings in a way that the other person can understand.

You also need to be able to listen to their point of view. With EFT, you can usually work through the emotions before trying to resolve the conflict. It can also help to look at it as if you are not personally involved, and try to see the situation from the perspective of a third person who is observing it from the outside.

IMPROVING YOUR RELATIONSHIPS WITH EFT AND GTT

The real key to improving your relationships is to move toward wholeness within yourself. Here are some suggestions on fulfilling your potential:

1. Start with EFT. At the end of each day, examine how you have related to those around you. Where you find anger, frustration, impatience, or other unresolved emotions, clear one or two emotions each day with EFT. This alone can transform your relationships and many problems will disappear.

2. Where you continue to experience conflict after using EFT, try the Holistic Process or the Unification Process. This will help you to understand more precisely what is happening within yourself and release the blockages you find.

3. If possible, have both parties use these processes to release the blockages that are preventing you from completely honoring each other. Discuss the results. This will help you to understand each other better and bring you closer.

4. Take a survey of your boundaries at the PEM&S levels. Write down any places where you are not in balance in your journal, and implement changes you need to return to wholeness. If you are having trouble communicating your needs, use EFT and GTT to release any fears related to speaking up.

5. Keep the lines of communication open. It is easier to resolve

small conflicts as they arise than it is to resolve emotions that have been building up for weeks or months.

Your Possibilities

Like many couples, we (Phillip and Jane) are very different individuals. Phillip takes an active approach to situations that come up in his life and responds quickly. Jane is more introspective. She tends to hold back for awhile and evaluate all of the possibilities. When we expect each other to respond the way we would individually, we are bound to be disappointed. If we open ourselves to the expanded perspective we have together, we both benefit. We have learned to be open-minded and both of us have grown as a result.

You may be amazed at how the relationships in your life change with regular use of EFT and GTT. You have the opportunity to look at those around you in a new way and to expand your possibilities. We plan to explore this subject in more depth in our upcoming book *Getting Thru to Those You Love*.

GRIEVING

The loss of a loved one is one of life's most challenging experiences. Grieving also provides one of our greatest opportunities for transformation.

The experience of a loss gives us valuable information about ourselves and our journey to wholeness.

The key is to find out what need the subject of the grief filled and to fill it oneself. In doing this, we reach a higher level of awareness. We can honor the other person and his or her contribution in our life. If it is not done, we may dig ourselves deeper into the hole of denial of the truth of who we are.

Grieving applies to any loss that creates a sense of separation from other people and things that provide us with love, security, and self-worth. It may be the result of a death, a divorce, a job layoff, and so on. Grieving may even involve the loss of possessions in a burglary, fire, or natural disaster. The way a person perceives a loss depends on how the lost person or object relates to his or her sense of self, her identity, and the needs the source of the grief filled.

OUR IDENTITIES

We have discussed the acknowledged parts of ourselves and the image we want to project. These parts form our identity or sense of self. Here are some examples:

- Many people identify themselves with their professions, like "I am a manager." In such cases, being laid off from this managerial position may bring out deeper problems than the loss of income. It may actually represent a loss of one's sense of self.

- Parents may identify themselves with their children, as with "I am Sarah's Mother". When the children move away, the parents' sense of self may go with them.

- People may identify themselves with their spouses, as "I am John William's wife." If the husband dies, the wife may have to re-examine who she really is.

- Some individuals may identify themselves with their physical appearance, and continuously grieve the loss of their youth.

- People may even identify themselves with their possessions, like a car, clothing, or piece of jewelry. In such cases, loss of possessions may be as significant as the loss of a close friend.

Here are some examples of needs a loved one may fill:

- A wife may rely on her husband for safety and security. When he is gone, she has to fill this need herself.

- A man may rely on his mother for nurturing. When she is gone, he needs to fill this need himself.

A powerful example for Jane was the loss of her mother, Lois, to Alzheimer's Disease. When it became apparent that Lois was no longer consciously with us, Jane had to go through the grieving process. In her sorrow, she recognized that Lois filled her need for unconditional love. She was the one person who was always there for her. Like many mothers, Lois was Jane's biggest supporter and always thought that everything she did was unique and special. With her loss, Jane realized that she had to provide this support for herself and found it to be a big order. She had to learn to love herself more.

The more a person is attached to someone or something for his or her sense of self, the greater the potential loss. In each case, the grieving experience is an opportunity to replace false identities and co-dependent needs with a deeper sense of the True Self. Grieving can help us to separate genuine love for another, which is unconditional, from false love based on dependency and neediness.

Aspects of Grieving

Here are some aspects of grieving to explore:

- **Denial:** We may repress the depth of our feelings of loss. When this happens, the unconscious feelings create a blockage that needs to be released to move into wholeness. One important aspect of grieving is to honor and embrace your feelings.

- **Anger:** A grieving person may blame a departed one for leaving him or her. This reaction is common in children, who are left feeling helpless. It is also found in people who feel insecure and depend on others to help them.

- **Guilt:** The grieving person may feel guilty for not having done enough for the other person. This reaction is found in people who are particularly concerned about meeting the needs of others. We need to be able to accept the past to move productively into the future.

- **Painful Memories:** In cases where the loss was painful, troubling memories may plague the grieving person. There is a process at the end of this chapter that can help with these memories or other painful images that come into your mind.

People often feel guilty about grieving the loss of a pet. Losing a pet may be more difficult than losing a person. It makes sense that we would miss a member of the family who is so close. Our pets may be with us most of the time, providing continuous love and support. We need to honor the profound roles they play in our lives.

USING EFT AND GTT WITH GRIEVING

Here are some ways that EFT and GTT can help you to complete the grieving process quickly and increase your awareness.

- You can start with EFT to reduce troubling emotions like pain, anger, and guilt. With these emotions, the ultimate goal is acceptance of yourself and what has happened. Grief can be so painful that it is buried away deep in the unconscious for weeks, months, or even longer. We have worked with people who continued to experience grief for many years after the loss of a loved one.

- Along with the painful emotions, you may need to deal with stress related to the events surrounding the loss. EFT is usually effective here as well.

- Once the preliminaries are out of the way, you can decide if your need to go deeper. You may already know the need the subject of the grief filled. If not, you can use the Holistic Process or the Unification Process to increase your awareness and provide a deeper level of healing.

- Grieving takes time. Some people may resist slowing down to avoid facing their feelings. You need to allow space for the feelings to come out, to transform them, and to integrate the experience. Journaling is also a good way to get in touch with the feelings.

In addition to learning from losses, there are profound lessons from the grieving process that we can incorporate into our daily lives This can help us to value our remaining relationships. Here are some suggestions:

- Take advantage of the opportunities you have to express your appreciation for those you love.

- Examine the needs others fill in your life that you need to begin to fill for yourself.

As the pain of grief releases, you have an opportunity to truly appreciate and honor the role the loved one played in your life. To complete the procedure, you can turn any painful memories into positive images that will come to mind whenever you remember your loved one.

THE REFRAMING PROCESS

When there is a loss, the grieving person may become stuck with memories of the difficult times rather than the good times. For example, a person who lost his mother to cancer may see her in pain on her dying bed when he thinks of her, rather than seeing an image of a positive time they had together. This happens because the unconscious mind records experiences in its own way and traumatic experiences often surface the most easily.

You can change this with reframing. The process provided here is a variation of techniques that are commonly used with Hypnotherapy and NLP. With the Reframing Process, you can re-program yourself to recall your most positive memories and regain the sense of closeness you felt at those times. The painful memories tend to cut you off from the subject of your loss. Even when a person has died, it is possible to retrieve the feelings of closeness you had when you were together.

You can use the Reframing Process for grieving or for dealing with any painful image that comes into your mind. The pictures that run through our minds have a profound effect on us. We are all familiar with the saying: "What you see is what you get." This is literally true. Images are like beliefs that have become three-dimensional.

As with the other processes in this book, you can close your eyes at any time to visualize and take a few breaths to deepen your experience. To make the most of it, read each word of the process slowly to yourself.

Start by taking a few deep breaths and allowing any tension you feel in your body to begin to melt away. Fill your lungs completely with pure, clear air with each inhale, and allow more tension to release with each exhale, so you feel more relaxed with each breath, and your body becomes lighter and lighter. Just allow any tension you are releasing to melt down through your body, legs and feet and into the earth. As you continue to breathe, allow the breath to be loving and nurturing, embracing yourself with relaxation. Focus on sending this relaxation to every part of your body, starting at the tip of your head and working your way down to the tips of your toes.

When you feel relaxed, allow your painful memory or image to come into your awareness. If it is uncomfortable, imagine that you are moving away from it until you feel better. As you continue to focus your awareness on the image, make note of what you see, how you feel physically, how you feel emotionally and what you hear. Focus particularly on how you feel emotionally and on how close or distant the other person feels. When you have a complete picture in your mind, set it aside and do some EFT if you need to release any painful emotions.

Now take a few deep breaths to clear your mind. Breathe in clear, loving energy, and allow yourself to recall a positive time. If you are focusing on a lost loved one, imagine a time when you were together. If you are focusing on another painful image, change to another time when you felt wonderful and happy. Focus all of your senses on this positive memory, making note of what you see, how you feel, and what you hear. Focus particularly on how you feel emotionally and on feelings of closeness between you. When the image is complete, ask yourself what color you would associate with this positive image, and surround the image with this color.

When the new image is complete, imagine that you can send the positive energy and the beautiful color over the painful image, then cover the entire image with the positive one, so the painful image disappears. Surround yourself with the color, and focus

again on the positive feelings, knowing that you can recall the
positive scene again at any time, bringing in the positive color,
feelings, and image you just experienced.

Now imagine that the future is extended out before you, and
send the positive color and feelings into your future to enrich your
entire life. As you gaze out into this future, remind yourself that
you will be able to recall the positive experience and all that you
have gained any time you wish in the future.

Take a few final breaths, breathing in active energy, feeling
you are ready to return to your normal state of awareness.

When this process is complete, you should be able to recall
the positive experience when you think of the subject of your
grief in the future. You can intensify this experience at any
time by focusing again on surrounding yourself with the feelings and the color you associated with the image. If another
painful memory surfaces, just repeat the procedure.

CAROL'S PROCESS:
GRIEVING THE LOSS OF HER HUSBAND

Jane worked with a client we will call Carol, who had recently
lost her husband, Neil, to cancer. During the final months of
his life, Carol cared for Neil at home, trying to keep him as
comfortable as possible, in spite of constant pain. After his
death, she had lingering memories of those difficult moments
and his fear of death.

Jane and Carol did the Reframing Process to help Carol to
change her perspective. When Carol started to focus on the
painful memories, she recalled several times when she was
with her husband. One time, she remembered preparing his
medications, knowing that they would not fully relieve the

pain. She felt a deep sadness, which she estimated to be around eight or nine in intensity.

With Jane's guidance, Carol did EFT on the sadness and brought it down to a one. They then went on to focus on a positive time. Carol recalled how she and Neil used to walk arm-in-arm. Thinking about it made her feel warm inside, and she could sense the love between them. After a moment, she experienced another wave of sadness for the loss of that closeness. This time the sadness was around a four and went away completely after a little more EFT.

With the sadness gone, Carol focused again on the image of her walking arm-in-arm with her husband. She could feel the closeness, and, this time, his love encompassed her without evoking any sadness. She could sense them surrounded by a beautiful yellow light, and heard the sounds of a gently babbling brook. She felt refreshed. At Jane's suggestion, Carol sent the yellow light over the painful image and transformed it.

The Reframing Process helped Carol to regain her feelings of closeness with Neil and release the sadness surrounding her loss. With this book, you now have more resources to make grieving a positive experience, where you can learn, clear and grow. The loss of a loved one is also one of life's most stressful experiences. We explore stress in the next part of the book.

WONDERFUL CHANGES

Have you ever felt that you could make some positive changes in your life, but you don't where to start? Taking that first step is one of the most difficult parts of any process. The purpose of the next part of the book is to give you some more ideas for using EFT and GTT.

In the EFT classes, one of our main goals is to help to expand our students' concepts of what they can do with these techniques. In Part 4, you will find out how EFT and GTT can help with some of the most common problems affecting millions of people in our country. If you have practiced the techniques in the first three parts of the book, you are ready for all of the chapters in Part 4.

Part 4

GETTING DOWN TO SPECIFICS

CHAPTER TEN
Eliminating Stress

*There is more to life
than increasing its speed.*

- MOHANDAS GANDHI

In our fast-paced society, stress affects millions of people. Being "stressed out" is such a common phenomenon, many consider it to be normal. Of course, the body views it differently.

What exactly causes stress? It is different for different people. A situation that is stimulating for one person may produce extreme discomfort in another. One person may find the thought of running a one-mile race exhilarating, while another finds it almost unbearably frightening. There are a number of reasons for these differences, and understanding them is beneficial to your well-being. Some factors to consider include:

- The balance between your physical constitution and the demands made on you.

- Results of pain or other physical conditions.

- Programmed responses learned from family, teachers, and other influential people.

- The presence of repressed emotions like hurt, anger, or grief.

- Prolonged exposure to difficult situations.

- How your circumstances relate to achieving your goals in life.

WHAT IS STRESS?

Stress is a response to an overwhelming stimulus that activates the body's fight or flight mechanism. This reaction is designed to bring a rapid end to the circumstances that have aroused the response. Unfortunately, it is frequently activated in situations that are not easily changed or withdrawn from, like while at work, with friends, or with family. In such cases, the stress response may become more of an ongoing condition than a momentary reaction.

Ongoing stress can have negative consequences both emotionally and physically, eventually weakening the immune system. EFT and GTT can help reduce stress, along with helping you to understand more about yourself and what the stress is trying to tell you. These techniques can produce tremendous benefits and reduce the need for medications.

The Nervous System

Physically, stress is a function of the autonomic nervous system. This system has two basic modes of operation, which are called the sympathetic nervous system and the parasympathetic nervous system. When awareness is focused on comfortable conditions that are not alarming to a person, the parasympathetic nervous system is operating. This system maintains balance within the body, and is able to restore it to a state of wellness when the balance has been interrupted.

The sympathetic nervous system, which is the fight or flight mechanism, goes into operation when the conditions become alarming or overwhelming. The reaction is the same when you are overwhelmed by the circumstances of your life or imagine being in danger, as it is when you are in a genuinely dangerous situation. The body responds immediately with more rapid breathing and heartbeat, a rise in blood pressure, a cessation of the digestive processes, and the secretion of adrenaline. These reactions are designed to put the body in a state of readiness to respond to imminent danger.

The sympathetic nervous system is only designed to operate for a short period of time, followed by a period of normalization by the parasympathetic nervous system. When people are in situations that are perceived to be alarming or dangerous for long periods of time, the sympathetic nervous system remains active, destroying the balance in the body. Over time, this can severely weaken or destroy the immune system. The frequent release of adrenaline can also cause insomnia and reduce a person's ability to relax even when circumstances normalize.

In cases where stress is affecting a person's health, overcoming it may be critical. In less severe cases, it is still a key factor in the quality of life.

Understanding how stress affects us can help us to understand ourselves at a deeper level and make the changes we need to have a healthy and joyful life.

Medical intervention can only be of limited value. Using prescription drugs to relieve stress deals with the physical

symptoms, not the real causes. There are also risks of side effects, which makes prolonged use impractical. With the techniques in this book, medications may be unnecessary.

REDUCING STRESS WITH EFT AND GTT

We will deal with the relationship between stress and insomnia, physical pain, and illness in more detail in the following
chapters. We begin here with the emotional, mental, and spiritual components of stress.

1. **Getting Started:** With increased awareness, most people can
   find ways to make simple changes that will reduce the stress in
   their daily lives.

   - **Evaluate the circumstances that are creating stress.** Re-
     view the regular activities of your life, and notice where the
     stress is coming from. Many of us are so busy, we are not
     even sure why we are feeling stressed. Write a comprehen-
     sive list of the stressful situations you commonly find your-
     self in. This new awareness is where healing begins.

   - **Change your responses to stressful circumstances.** Once
     you have a list of the stressful circumstances in your life,
     you can begin to work on them with EFT. As you go down
     the list and reduce the emotional responses that are creat-
     ing the stress, you will find yourself in a more balanced
     state, where you can be more resourceful. This should also
     demonstrate the generalization effect. After going through a
     few of the circumstances on your list, the others will proba-
     bly seem less stressful. At some point, all of the items on
     the list may be neutralized.

2. **Bringing Your Life into Balance:** When you begin to feel bet-

ter, you may want to stop there. We recommend going further, because it is likely that ongoing exposure to the same stressful situations will cause the emotions to re-appear. You may also need to make some changes to bring your life into balance.

- **Find ways to reduce outside pressures.** Most Americans lead very active lives. This focus on achievement is a major element in our programming as a society. When asked "What did you do today," most of us feel compelled to produce a list of accomplishments that justify our existence. Often, we are motivated by a strong sense of obligation or concern about what other people think of us. Both relate to insecurity and low self-esteem. When we fully accept ourselves, we are not motivated by what other people think about what we do. Instead, we are drawn forward by a genuine desire to manifest our Soul's purpose in life.

  People who are not able to accept themselves as they are may try to prove themselves through their accomplishments. This type of low self-esteem motivates workaholics and over-achievers. In the holistic model, these are two examples of fragmented personalities that need to be reunited with the Soul to create balance.

  Once you have reduced the emotional charge with EFT, you may want to use GTT to examine the parts of yourself who create unnecessary pressure. Go over your list again, and identify where wounded parts of yourself are at work. Using the Unification Process, you can bring these parts of yourself into balance and find new ways to organize your life.

- **Develop new responses to circumstances that are to remain.** Sometimes we allow outside influences to create stress unnecessarily. If we have not focused on developing healthy responses to the situations we encounter, we may be victims to the random programming of the unconscious mind. We may allow things to bother us unnecessarily.

There are obviously many things we cannot change, like driving in heavy traffic. The drivers around you may be rude, aggressive, impatient, and thoughtless, but you have a choice of whether to allow them to bother you or not. Relaxing music and a new attitude can work wonders. You can develop similar strategies for dealing with other small irritations in your life, like waiting in lines, dealing with telemarketers, and so on. And you may be able to find ways to take a few moments for yourself during the day. Just taking a few deep breaths and walking around a bit may make a big difference.

- **Find more ways to incorporate relaxation and pleasure into your life.** We have already seen how our society is oriented toward action and accomplishment. To achieve true balance, you also need to include relaxation and pleasure on a daily basis. This may include doing a regular relaxation process or meditation, walking in nature, taking an occasional bubble bath, having a relaxing massage, allowing an extra ten minutes to get where you need to go, and maybe taking a more scenic route.

  EFT can help here, too. If you cannot shut off the constant chattering in your mind, you can use EFT to help you to let go, so you can relax more deeply. Frequently, there is a fragmented part that is afraid of letting go or losing control that needs to be dealt with so that you can enjoy life more. Whatever the cause of the chatter is, ask yourself why your mind does not want to let go and proceed from there.

PROGRESSIVE RELAXATION

Relaxation techniques can produce amazing results with many conditions. According to Dr. Bernie Siegel in his book *Peace, Love and Healing*:

> You can use relaxation training, for example, to lower blood pressure, slow your breath and heart rates and reduce muscle tension. ...Studies have shown that relaxation training and related techniques can be helpful in combating the negative effects of prolonged stress on the immune system components. A dys-regulated immune system can affect everything from your susceptibility to colds to your ability to kill cancer cells or AIDS viruses and may also be a factor in asthma, allergies, diabetes, multiple schlorosis, rheumatoíd, arthritis, lupus and other auto-immune diseases in which the body attacks itself. ...Relaxation is so commonly acknowledged to be effective that some hospitals now broadcast relaxation programs on closed circuit television in the patient's rooms. The list of diseases altered in a positive way by relaxation would fill this page.

The Progressive Relaxation Process is simple and effective. It shows how easily you can change your state by bringing awareness to your breath and your body. Before starting, take a moment to make a note of how you feel physically, emotionally, and mentally. Find a quiet spot for yourself and you are ready. Just read each word of the process slowly to yourself, and close your eyes whenever you want to go deeper.

Begin by shifting your focus from your mind to your body. Notice how you feel where you are sitting or lying and notice how your breath feels as you inhale and exhale. In a moment we will ask you to stop reading, close your eyes, and take a few deep, deep breaths. As you do this, you can imagine that the tension in your body is beginning to melt and is gently drifting down your arms and legs, melting out through the tips of your fingers and the bottoms of your feet into the earth. Allow the breath to go all the way down through your body, feeling your stomach freely expand and contract with each breath, as you completely fill your lungs with pure, fresh air. Close your eyes for a moment now, and focus on taking a few deep breaths.

And now, as you continue to breathe, do it in a loving way, nourishing and nurturing yourself with each breath, feeling loving energy flowing throughout your body. Focus on bringing this pure energy into your mind with each inhale, so that all of the cells of your brain can relax and any thoughts from the day can drift off into the air. Notice how your mind becomes clearer and clearer with each breath. Now allow the pure energy to move down so that your entire head is relaxed, including your forehead, eyebrows, jaw, mouth and chin. Feel the energy traveling down your neck and shoulders, again allowing any tension in these areas to simply melt away so that your neck and shoulders can feel completely relaxed.

Now allow a wave of clear energy and relaxation to move gently down your arms, past the elbows and wrists, all the way to the tips of your fingers. And feel another wave of relaxation moving down from your shoulders so that your entire torso can relax, and all of the organs in your body can relax. Feel the energy moving down the chest, relaxing the lungs and heart, the stomach and down past the waist, allowing your abdomen to relax. Now feel the relaxation moving all the way down your spine, so that your entire back can relax, melting further into your chair. And allow the relaxation to move down the thighs, to the knees, the ankles and feet, all the way to the tips of your toes, so your entire body is relaxed and filled with clear, pure energy. Now focus for a moment on sending pure energy and love throughout your body. And ask yourself: Is there a particular part of your body that is harder to love than another part? If you feel that there is, ask yourself why? And now, simply send more of the loving energy to that part. Or if you feel tension or pain in a specific area, send energy with your breath to that part of the body and allow the pain to release. This is something you can also explore by journaling, writing down your thoughts and feelings. Allow the different parts of your body to talk to you. What do they have to say? What do they need from you?

You can stay in this relaxed state and breathe pure fresh air for as long as you wish, closing your eyes and sending energy into all of the areas of your body from the top of your head to the tip of your toes.

When you are ready to return, just focus on breathing in more active energy to bring you back to your normal waking state, feeling yourself firmly connected to the ground beneath you, and feeling wonderful.

Notice how you feel now compared with how you felt before you started. You will probably perceive differences at all levels.

After experiencing progressive relaxation, you may feel free of stress. You can return to this peaceful state as you face life's inevitable challenges. You may want to go through this procedure a few times, until you can use it to feel more relaxed without the script. It is so simple, you can do it almost anywhere. With practice, you will find yourself relaxing more easily, so you can bring yourself back into balance any time.

Now we will focus on another condition that often goes hand-in-hand with stress: insomnia.

CHAPTER ELEVEN

Overcoming Insomnia

How beautiful it is to do nothing,
and then rest afterwards.

- SPANISH PROVERB

Having regular, restful sleep is an integral part of your overall well-being. The inability to sleep soundly and restfully takes its toll on our moods and the physical body. With the complexity of modern life, millions of Americans suffer from sleep-related problems. In fact, the April 1999 edition of the *Harvard Men's Health Watch* estimates that about 40 million Americans suffer from insomnia, and that many of these people consider it to be among their greatest personal problems. In addition to being frustrating and interfering with their daytime activities, insomnia or restless sleep can have long-range effects on their health.

In the last chapter, we discussed how the autonomic nervous system maintains balance within the body through the functioning of the parasympathetic nervous system. When this system is functioning properly, we can easily repair and restore the body to a state of wellness. But when we are not able to sleep restfully, the parasympathetic nervous system is missing one of its best opportunities to do its work, leaving the body vulnerable to physical problems.

Many people who have insomnia rely on sedatives to induce sleep. As mentioned before, medications can relieve the symptoms, but they do not address the cause, which is what we need to do to reestablish the natural rhythms and balance of the body. Anyone who has taken sleeping pills also knows that their use does not produce the same rejuvenating effect that natural sleep has on the body. Instead of waking up feeling refreshed and ready to begin a new day, the body feels the residues of the drugs. As a result, the user's health may suffer, both from interruption of the natural functioning of the body and the side effects from the sedatives.

Here are some reasons why sleep may be disrupted:

- Stress and anxiety.
- Worrying about problems.
- Depression.
- Pain and discomfort.
- Irregular sleeping habits.
- Bad dreams.

To add to this list, a period of insomnia may program the mind to go to bed with a fear of not being able to sleep, which further intensifies the problem. In most cases, EFT can help to release the emotions that prevent a person from getting restful sleep. Often, this is all that is needed.

If you have insomnia that is linked with stress, refer also to the suggestions in Chapter Ten. You will need to deal with the stress to overcome the insomnia.

CONNECTING WITH THE INNER INSOMNIAC

If EFT alone has not corrected your insomnia, you can turn to the use of GTT to get to the heart of the problem. Sometimes the causes are immediately apparent, sometimes not. From our experience, insomnia is frequently linked to an over-active mind. For some reason, the mind is unable to let go enough to relax completely. With one of our clients, the problem went all the way back to her childhood. Her parents had such high expectations of her, she felt that she always had to be mentally alert, fearing that something might go wrong if she let go even for a moment. The fear was so extreme that she was unable to allow her mind to relax enough to get a good night's sleep. With just a little EFT and GTT, she was able to sleep with ease for the first time in years.

With the Unification Process, you can find out what your problem is and start on the way to getting restful sleep.

CHAPTER TWELVE

Relieving Pain

Although the world is full of suffering,
it is full also of overcoming it.

- HELEN KELLER

For most of us, the mere mention of pain produces stress and fear. We have been trained to regard it as an enemy to be avoided at all costs. Actually, the opposite is true. Pain is the body's way of getting our attention. When understood holistically, it is telling us that something is wrong. This is valuable information. It prompts us to give ourselves the attention we need to bring ourselves back into balance, which is, of course, the goal in any healing process.

The source of pain may be physical, but we have seen how everything is connected, so there are generally aspects of it on the EM&S levels as well. Healing these levels may reduce or completely eliminate the pain. For example, we all know that headaches, stomach problems, and muscular tensions are frequently stress-related. If you can deal with the stress, the physical symptoms may disappear, too.

Most Americans are affected by pain at some time in their lives. In his book *Healing Back Pain*, John E. Sarno, MD, reports that around 80 percent of the population has a history of pain associated with the back, neck, shoulders, buttocks and limbs. He considers it to be largely a psychological condition. In 1986, Forbes magazine reported that $56 billion was spent annually on this condition, so the amount is certainly much higher today. Back pain is also a major cause of job absenteeism and the second major reason for doctor visits.

Dr. Sarno has taken what many consider a radical approach in his treatment of these conditions, with overwhelming success. First he rules out a physical reason for the pain, which only occurs in a small minority of his cases. Then he treats the remaining patients on the emotional and mental levels for a condition he calls TMS (Tension Myositis Syndrome).

Interestingly, Dr. Sarno's physical diagnosis excludes the structural abnormalities that most people associate with back pain, like slipped disks. From his experience, most people have structural abnormalities, but he has found no direct relationship between these problems and the types of pain his patients experience. Using this approach, Dr. Sarno has reported complete success in between eighty and ninety percent of his patients, and partial success in many of the rest. In the most recent survey mentioned in his book, only two percent remained unchanged.

Dr. Sarno's book is an enlightening statement on how our thoughts, emotions, and bodies are connected. He associates TMS with the repression of emotions like anxiety, stress, and anger, along with mental conditioning. He says that his patients always start out believing that the pain is associated with a specific event, like an auto accident, a sports injury, or lifting the wrong way. But when he helps them to examine what else was happening when the pain started, they recall other major events, like getting married, starting a new job, having a financial setback, or dealing with an illness or death in the family.

As we have seen in our exploration of the unconscious mind, we frequently repress our feelings associated with traumatic events out of an inability to deal with them effectively. In the cases Dr. Sarno cites, the repressed emotions show up as physical pain. When his patients are educated about what is happening, almost all of them get better.

As a note, Dr. Sarno has found that other physical conditions are linked with the repression of emotions just like TMS. His list includes ulcers, hernias, asthma, hay fever, headaches, eczema, psoriasis, spastic colon and irritable bowel syndrome.

ENLISTING THE BODY'S HEALING SYSTEM

Many people take extreme measures to avoid and quickly eliminate pain. In their rush to eliminate the discomfort, they ignore the underlying causes. Unfortunately, medication can only be used safely for a limited period of time and may have dangerous side effects. EFT and GTT provide safe alternatives. EFT alone often works quickly and effectively with pain. You can also take the process a step further and uncover the emotions, beliefs, and judgments that are connected with the pain. Sometimes, you may know what is behind your pain. When this is not the case, you can find out with the Holistic Process.

EFT and GTT both enlist the body's healing system. When the energy system is brought into balance, messages sent from our brain via neurotransmitters can stimulate the body's production of chemicals that help to relieve symptoms and, in some cases, produce positive physical changes as well. Dr.

Deepak Chopra describes this in his book *Quantum Healing*:

> We already know that the living body is the best pharmacy ever devised. It produces diuretics, painkillers, tranquilizers, sleeping pills, antibiotics and indeed everything manufactured by the drug companies, but it makes them much, much better. The dosage is always right and given on time; side effects are minimal or non-existent; and the directions for using the drug are included in the drug itself, as part of its built-in intelligence.

SPECIAL CONDITIONS

We have already explained that EFT and GTT are not substitutes for proper medical treatment. We have also seen how beneficial they can be when they are included along with medical treatment, with the consent of the physician.

In addition to viewing pain as a response to a physical condition, we need to examine how the brain perceives it. People respond differently to pain, based on their programming. Our families show us how to react to pain from a young age. For a child whose only way of getting attention is pain, he or she may unconsciously learn to use aches and pains to enlist support from others. This may continue into adulthood, making pain an unconscious call for attention.

Our responses to pain may also depend on the external circumstances. When we are about to leave on vacation, a little pain may go unnoticed. When we return from the vacation and are preparing to go back to work, the same pain may become almost unbearable. This type of response is surprisingly common. Doctors even report an increase in heart attacks on Monday mornings. Some factors to consider:

- Your physical constitution and current condition.

- Your background and how your family relates to pain.

- Your current circumstances and major events in your life.

- The levels of stress and fear you experience in your daily life.

Interestingly, pain may actually have no physical basis at all. People with amputated arms or legs report pain in areas where the limbs have been removed.

JOANN'S PROCESS: LOWER BACK PAIN

In one of our classes, we had a student we will call Joann, who had suffered for 19 years with pressure on the lower left side of her back. We did the Holistic Process to find out what was happening. As Joann focused on the pressure, she became aware of feelings of betrayal and rejection related to a divorce she had gone through around the time her back pain started. She also felt resentment about having devoted all of her energy to the marriage. When it ended, she was left to fend for herself, without having developed any skills to support herself. Mentally, her lack of career training left her feeling powerless. Spiritually, she felt rejected and unloved.

We did EFT on the rejection. It started at a six and went down to a two or three after one round. After doing the Floor-to-Ceiling Eye Roll, the rejection was completely gone, and all of the pressure was gone from her back. She mentioned that she could feel movement there as her energy reconfigured.

SURGERY, CHILDBIRTH, AND DENTAL WORK

EFT and GTT can be effective additions to standard medical procedures where fear of pain and other types of discomfort may complicate the process. Thousands of people have such extreme fear of going to the dentist that they never go or are unable to get through the door when they arrive at the dentist's office. Using EFT and GTT before procedures like childbirth, surgery, and dental work can reduce stress and help to stimulate the body's ability to clear. Some considerations to explore with EFT and GTT:

- Your emotions and thoughts about the process.
- Fear of losing control.
- Fear of death.

When you are at the dentist, a doctor's office, or the hospital, you can also do the Progressive Relaxation Process in Chapter Ten to help stay relaxed and take your mind off the procedure at hand. Even just taking a few deep breaths can work wonders.

With pregnancy and childbirth, you may also want to look beyond the physical components of medical procedures. Expecting a baby can bring up concerns for both the mother and father. Addressing these issues before the birth can be a tremendous help. Here are some examples:

- Concerns associated with having a child such as finances, relationships, and so on.
- Concerns about having adequate parenting skills.
- Fear associated with the birth experience.

With any medical procedure, you may have fragmented parts that need to be reintegrated with the Unification Process. This can bring deeper meaning to the birth experience, ease fears, and facilitate healing in any medical procedure.

THE BIRTH EXPERIENCE

From the perspective of the baby, we have also found that the prenatal period and the birth experience are critical times in a person's life. Birth is one of the most important experiences we have, which also makes it a time when we are highly programmable.

Imagine the excited baby making his grand debut. How do you think he would feel if uncaring hands removed him, slapped a few times on the rear, and then set aside unceremoniously on a stainless steel scale? Most births are being handled with more sensitivity now, but many of us were born in a time when there was little awareness of the experience from the baby's point-of-view.

Most people's awareness of being in the womb and being born is completely unconscious, but these experiences affect us nonetheless. We have worked with a number of people who were aware on an unconscious level of being unwanted before they were born. As you might imagine, this can leave deep feelings of guilt and low self-esteem. Similarly, if something goes wrong during the birth, a person may be traumatized for life. We worked with one woman who was caught in the birth canal and extracted in a very painful way. She was left with tremendous anger and distrust of people in general. She also had neck pain that was related to the trauma of being twisted during the process.

If you are wondering whether you were affected by prenatal or birth trauma, close your eyes for a moment, and focus on the time of your birth, or the time you were in the womb. Take a few deep breaths and notice how you feel. This should give you an idea. If you feel any painful emotions, it is likely that something happened that still needs to be addressed. If so, you may be able to go through it with the Holistic Process or the Unification Process. We also offer assistance. You can find out more about the services we provide at the end of this book.

Having an understanding of how our emotions affect an unborn child also provides a compelling reason to seek balance within ourselves during pregnancy. Clearing imbalances related to the birth experience will help the process go more smoothly for the entire family.

We also have to accept the fact that pain is a part of each of our lives from the time we are born until we die. Most of us treat it like an unwelcome relative, trying to get rid of it as soon as possible. Now you can relate to pain in a positive way. With the processes in this book, you can understand what your body is trying to tell you, and lead a more harmonious life.

CHAPTER THIRTEEN

Creating Physical Well-being

*The natural healing force
within each one of us
is the greatest force in getting well.*

- HIPPOCRATES

The discovery of neurotransmitters, the minute chemicals that transmit impulses between the brain and the nerve cells, immune system cells and the organs of the body, has provided scientific evidence of what many people already knew: Our minds and our bodies are connected. Our beliefs, attitudes, thoughts, and emotions have a direct impact on our physical well-being.

EFT provides further evidence. As Gary Craig mentions in his *EFT Manual*:

Applying EFT for emotional issues often brings on the cessation of physical problems. Breathing problems go away. Headaches vanish. Joint pains subside. Multiple sclerosis symptoms improve. I have witnessed this phenomenon for years. The list of physical improvements brought about by EFT is endless.

Endless though it may be, he provides this list:

[P]hysical ailments which have been addressed with EFT with either partial or complete success: headaches, back pain, stiff neck and shoulders, joint pains, cancer, chronic fatigue syndrome, lupus, ulcerative colitis, psoriasis, asthma, allergies, itching eyes, body sores, rashes, insomnia, constipation, irritable bowel syndrome, eyesight, muscle tightness, bee stings, urination problems, morning sickness, PMS, sexual dysfunctions, sweating, poor coordination, carpal tunnel syndrome, arthritis, numbness in the fingers, stomachaches, toothaches, trembling, multiple sclerosis.

Interestingly, many of these conditions are the same ones we mentioned in the last chapter where we reported the findings of Dr. John Sarno. Though he specializes in dealing in back pain, he has found that a number of other physical conditions have a psychological origin.

FOCUSING ON WELL-BEING

Both doctors and their patients are beginning to shift their focus from curing symptoms to taking preventive measures to maintain physical health and well-being. For many years, most of us Americans have relied on doctors to take care of our physical conditions, without becoming actively involved or taking any personal responsibility. Instead, doctors have used medications to create well-being. When we had headaches, they prescribed pain pills. If we were overweight, they prescribed diet pills. If we felt depressed, they prescribed tranquilizers.

Time has shown that this approach is not working. Millions of people are in pain, overweight, depressed, and unhappy. We are also seeing that the side effects of the drugs we put in our bodies can be dangerous. We are beginning to take more responsibility for ourselves from a holistic perspective. We understand the importance of taking proper care of the body, along with the emotional, mental, and spiritual levels of ourselves that directly affect our overall wellness.

Dr. Bernie Siegel defines healing as creating the foundation on the emotional, mental, and spiritual levels within which the physical body can be cured medically. By clearing blockages on these levels, EFT and GTT can help you to create the proper environment for maintaining your physical well-being, or when a physical condition presents itself, for creating a positive environment for a physical recovery along with proper medical care.

Historically, there has been some recognition of these connections between the body and the mind with what is termed psychosomatic illness. Unfortunately, the word psychosomatic implies weakness and instability. Some people even understand it to mean that the illness is imaginary. Not surprisingly, many people are reluctant to consider the possibility that there may be an emotional, mental, or even spiritual component of their condition. Nonetheless, Dr. Christine Page, another physician who is exploring mind-body medicine, attests in her book *Frontiers of Health* that many of her patients can readily identify what was happening with them psychologically when their physical conditions developed.

When understood holistically, all of our physical problems exist for a reason: to show us something about ourselves.

This does not mean that we are bad, weak, or emotionally unstable. It simply means that everything is connected and that there is something to be gained from the experience. In *Peace, Love and Healing*, Dr. Bernie Siegel describes disease as a metaphor with a message that we need to hear. "Often the message will speak to us of our path and how we have strayed from it, so that our life is no longer a true expression of the inner self...."

He is referring to the development of the fragmented parts of ourselves who have been cut off from the Soul. When this happens, our ability to heal is impaired. Dr. Siegel further states: "True healers know the value of afflictions and of adversity. They know that within the symbolic experience of disease lies a path to change and self healing and a healthy bodymind."

Numerous studies have explored the affects of placebos, which are harmless substances used to produce positive changes in physical symptoms. At least 30 percent of the population responds positively to placebos. This alone demonstrates the power the mind has on the functioning of the body.

Unfortunately the opposite is also true, such as when a physician estimates that a patient has only six months to live. This death sentence is known as a "nocebo," and studies also indicate that a physician's realistic prognosis may actually hinder the patient's ability to overcome disease. When viewed as programming, the prognosis may actually cause the person to die as predicted. This occurs because many people are easily programmed by authority figures and see doctors as being ultimate authorities on their health.

CREATING WELL-BEING WITH EFT AND GTT

EFT and GTT are powerful tools for establishing and maintaining well-being. The obvious place to start is with using

EFT directly on physical symptoms. You can even do this even when you cannot measure the intensity on a scale of one to ten. Just say, "This _____." For example, if you have constipation, you can tap for "this constipation." You can also tailor your approach to the type of condition you are dealing with:

1. **Chronic** is defined as "referring to a disease or disorder that develops slowly and persists for a long period of time. It can sometimes remain for the person's lifetime." Chronic conditions often relate to core patterns of emotions, beliefs and judgments, and deep aspects of the Self. Here are some suggestions for dealing with chronic conditions:

   • If you are comfortable using Kinesiology, start by addressing "The Levels of Psychological Reversal" described in Figure 5.1. With chronic conditions, you will generally find PR. In such cases, if you find that you do not want to overcome your condition or do not believe that you deserve to overcome the condition, you certainly will not. We also recommend reading the section of Chapter 17 entitled "Switched Circuit." This condition is frequently present with chronic conditions.

   • Use the Holistic Process to uncover the emotions, beliefs and judgments related to the condition. This is particularly helpful if you have a weak muscle test response to any of the levels of PR. Addressing the exact nature of the PR and tapping for the emotion behind the condition provides a deeper level of healing. You may get noticeable results more quickly than tapping for the physical condition itself.

   • Set up a schedule and perform EFT regularly, at least once or twice a day. You may experience some relief immediately, but if not, persistence can produce results over time.

Experiences reported with EFT for these types of conditions indicate that you may notice changes over a period of weeks or months rather than days.

2. **Acute** is defined as "begins quickly and is intense or sharp, then slowing after a short time; sharp or severe." It generally refers to a recent disturbance or injury. This type of condition may respond more quickly to EFT, because the associated message may be more immediate and easy to integrate. You can make the changes you need to return quickly to a state of wellness. Here are some suggestions for dealing with acute conditions:

- From our extensive use of the Holistic Process and the Unification Process, we have found that acute conditions usually relate to things you need to understand about yourself now. For example, accidents often metaphorically represent a call for immediate attention to something that is happening in your life.

  This interpretation is difficult for some people to believe. Fortunately you do not have to believe anything we say to achieve positive results with EFT and GTT. Nonetheless, your results when dealing with acute conditions will probably be better if you can uncover the associated emotions, beliefs, and judgments with the Holistic Process. If you tap for the emotions and address the beliefs and judgments in the affirmation, you are likely to get results immediately or within a short time. The body is calling for your attention, and you are responding.

3. **Intermittent** is defined as "alternating between periods of activity and inactivity." This includes symptoms like headaches, asthma attacks and other disorders that come and go. Here are some suggestions for dealing with intermittent conditions:

- The appearance of intermittent symptoms often corresponds to the return of a recurring stimulus. For instance, anxiety may bring on an asthma attack. Or increased stress may bring on recurring back pain. The symptoms are trying to tell you something. It is most helpful to find out what your body is trying to tell you, so you can respond appropriately.

- Since intermittent symptoms relate to a specific part of your self, or subpersonality, you may want to use the Unification Process to connect with this part and find out exactly what he or she needs.

If you are not yet familiar enough with the procedures in this book to use the Holistic Process or Kinesiology, don't let that stop you. As you continue to master the processes, try EFT on the physical symptoms and any emotions that bother you regularly. Gary Craig has numerous case histories of people using EFT successfully with physical conditions on his Web site. See Appendix C.

Here are a few examples from Craig's files:

- A woman named Carolyn with lupus attended a one-hour seminar where Craig gave a brief introduction of his techniques and a few demonstrations of a short version of the process. Lupus is a condition that caused her hands and feet to become swollen. After attending the seminar, Carolyn decided to use EFT several times a day and her swelling subsided. She also experienced a rise in her vitality level, and the only thing she had done differently was to use EFT.

- Val suffered from migraines for ten years. She had tried everything she could think of, and, at wit's end, decided to try a session with an EFT practitioner. With his help, she was able to relate the onset of the migraines to her guilt over a difficult divorce, and learned how to use EFT. Three months after the session, she reported complete freedom. Craig has had success with headaches of all kinds.

- Andrea had suffered from constant pelvic pain and nausea for months before having a session with Gary. After achieving partial success with EFT alone, they explored the emotions behind the pain. Andrea felt remorse from a miscarriage, which corresponded to the onset of the nausea and pelvic pain. After releasing the remorse with EFT, the nausea and pain were completely gone. Ten days later, they had not returned.

As we mentioned before, we do not recommend substituting EFT for medical professional, but it can be a helpful addition when it is used with your doctor's permission.

ENGAGING YOUR INNER HEALER

The Unification Process provides a powerful way to bring more awareness to any physical problem you experience. It also allows you to connect directly with your healing system. When you contact your Ideal Healthy Self, you are connecting with the part of you who understands how to create well-being. People sometimes experience this part of themselves as an Inner Doctor or Wise Person who can show them how to be truly healthy.

Dr. Bemie Siegel says:

[J]ust as your eyes and your ears and the rest of your five senses are there to protect you from the world, so you have a sixth sense, your healing system, which is meant to repair injuries and protect you from invasion by bacteria, viruses and diseases.

With GTT, you can communicate with this healing system.

IMAGINING YOURSELF WELL

If you have a physical problem, along with EFT and GTT, you can imagine yourself well throughout the day. In *Imagery in Healing*, Jeanne Achterburg cites studies showing the direct effect imagination has on the body. She describes how it can influence processes as varied as muscle tension, salivation, heart rate, skin resistance, respiration, blood glucose, gastrointestinal activity, blister formation, and blood pressure. These effects include changes in both the musculoskeletal system and the involuntary nervous system, which we normally think of as being beyond our control.

With a little practice, it is easy for most people to visualize themselves healing and increasingly healthy. Children are particularly skilled in this area, because they have active imaginations. They can easily activate their inner senses to picture, hear, smell, touch, or taste anything they focus their attention on. If you feel stuck, it can help to approach it as an imaginative child would, without self-doubt and judgment.

To open to your deeper levels of awareness, start with one of the relaxation processes in this book. Then close your eyes and ask yourself for an image that can help you to correct a condition you are concerned about. If you have done the Unification Process on your health, you can connect with your Inner Healer for help. Use your imagination. For example, if you have a problem with digestion, you can visualize how food goes through your system from the time it enters your mouth until it is completely digested. As you visualize the food digesting, focus on how it is being absorbed easily and how the digested particles are providing nourishment to all of the cells of your body.

As you move toward creating wellness, you may also want to explore your weight, any addictive habits you have, and your need for physical exercise. The next three chapters address bringing all of them into balance.

CHAPTER FOURTEEN

Stopping Smoking and Other Habits

*It is not easy to find happiness in ourselves
and it is not possible to find it elsewhere.*

- AGNES REPPLIER

We all know that smoking is dangerous to our health. The United States Health Department reports that smokers tend to die five to ten years earlier than non-smokers. It is also increasingly expensive and inconvenient, with more and more public places becoming smoke-free. Nonetheless, over forty million Americans smoke.

Statistics show that most smokers would like to stop, but feel unable to do so. Many other people are plagued by similar habits and addictions that they feel incapable of breaking. These habits range from minor irritants like nail biting and nervous fidgeting to the use of caffeine to the use of destructive drugs and alcohol.

With these statistics, it is clear that conventional techniques for changing undesirable habits and addictions, like gathering your willpower and "toughing it out," don't work for most people. This approach does not address the cause of the behavior. If you are strong enough to tough it out in one area, like smoking, the addiction is likely to show up somewhere else, like in your weight. Similarly, people who overcome addictions to alcohol often become heavy smokers. The next chapter provides more specifics on weight issues. The information and suggestions provided here also apply to eating.

WHAT CAUSES ADDICTIONS?

Dr. Callahan provided a simple explanation for the cause of all addictions: anxiety. In each case, the habit or addiction provides a way to mask or subdue the underlying anxiety. This explanation addresses the emotional level. To complete the process, we also want to look at the mental and spiritual levels.

Holistically, addictive behavior is a misguided search for wholeness and balance. Spiritually, a person is drawn to a habit or addictive substance because something is missing inside. It ultimately comes down to loving oneself (refer to the levels of healing in Figure 2.1). On the mental level, different substances fill different needs. Our beliefs and attitudes determine how we relate to the world around us. The addictive thought system is a compulsive search for wholeness in people, things, and substances. From this perspective, alcohol often satisfies the desire to escape reality and caffeine fulfills the drive to increase performance. Figure 14.1 provides examples of some of the needs different substances fill.

To achieve genuine healing, releasing an addiction includes releasing the anxiety, the limiting beliefs, and the judgments

---

FIGURE 14.1
ADDICTIVE SUBSTANCES AND ISSUES

The following are examples of common issues on the emotional and mental levels that are associated with different addictive substances. Spiritually, the desire to seek fulfillment outside of oneself covers up the emptiness, lack of love, and low self-esteem on the inside.

SUBSTANCE	EMOTIONAL OR MENTAL ISSUE
Tobacco	• Sooth uneasiness in social situations • Relieve stress • Prove maturity, "adult" thing to do
Alcohol	• Remove inhibitions • Satisfy desire to escape reality • Forget about stresses and worries • Prove maturity, "adult" thing to do • Find way to be social
Food	• Soothe emotions • Protect self from sexuality • Protect self from being hurt
Caffeine	• Increase stamina
Marijuana	• Escape reality, similar to alcohol
Cocaine, Amphetamines	• Increase performance
Psychedelic Drugs	• Search for expansion of consciousness

that prevent us from loving ourselves just as we are. In his delightful book, *Healing the Addictive Mind*, Lee Jampolsky defines recovery from addiction as the process of awakening to love. When we experience ourselves as whole and balanced, addiction does not occur; we are complete.

OTHER CONSIDERATIONS

Here are two more considerations with habits and addictions:

1. **Society's Influence:** The external search for gratification and happiness is pervasive in our society. This is how most of us have been taught to live. Some of the ways our society influences us are as follows:

   - We have an abundance of food, alcohol, and other addictive substances, along with plenty of money to spend on them.

   - Modern life is stressful, removed from nature, and devoid of spirituality.

   - Our society is mind-oriented, not body-oriented. Bringing awareness and respect back to the body can be a transformational experience. People with harmful addictions are often unwilling to admit that they are mistreating their bodies. Anyone who loves his or her body will not abuse it in this way.

   - We are encouraged to use substances through advertising, TV, movies, and what we see around us in our daily lives.

2. **Denial:** Denial is an integral part of many addictions: laying the blame on other people ("My mother drove me to drink."), difficult circumstances ("I just need these tranquilizers to get through my divorce. Then I will be fine."), and so on.

Until a person is able to move beyond this stage and take responsibility for himself, he will not change. This is one of the main reasons why it is so important for the individual to change on his own volition, rather than through the begging of a spouse, parent, or friend. The addicted person has to come to the place where he can freely admit that there is a problem and commit to change.

BREAKING THE SMOKING HABIT

With our increasing awareness of the benefits of being smoke-free, chemical-free and so on, more and more people are looking for ways to overcome their addictions and habits. EFT has helped many people. Here are some of the things it can do:

- Reduce cravings.

- Release emotional patterns that feed the desire for the substance or behavior.

- Remove the fear of failure and increase the belief in success.

> *A holistic approach to habits and addictions reaches beyond the physical and emotional levels to find out exactly what is happening.*

GTT can help you bring awareness to what is occurring, so you feel prepared to make a firm commitment to change. This is important. The key ingredients to success in changing any undesirable habit or addiction are desire and commitment. When the cravings come, you have to commit to using EFT instead of succumbing to the object of your desire. Fortunately,

EFT is effective with all kinds of cravings.

EFT PROCESS REDUCING CRAVINGS

Whether you crave chocolate, cigarettes, or other substances, or have a nervous behavior like nail biting, you can use this technique to reduce your desire and loosen the hold of the habit. We will use a cigarette in this example, but you can substitute the substance of your choice.

1. Hold an unlit cigarette in your hand. Look at it, smell it, and put it in you mouth like you are planning to smoke it. Allow yourself to build a desire for it. Notice how the desire feels.

2. When you feel the craving, you are ready to do EFT. Measure its intensity from one to ten, then go through the short tapping sequence using "this craving" in the affirmation and the reminder phrase. If necessary, repeat the tapping or other EFT techniques, if required, until you are at zero or as close as you can come to zero. This usually works, but if you are unable to come close to zero using EFT alone, you can use the Unification Process to find out what is in your way.

3. When the desire for the cigarette, other substance, or behavior is as low as you can get it, notice how you feel about it now. Most people experience something between being neutral and feeling repulsion for the thing they strongly desired just a few moments earlier.

Usually, the craving will return later and you will need to repeat the process. Over time, the cravings will disappear altogether. Most cravings are substantially reduced the first day you use EFT, and become milder and less frequent as the days pass. The important thing is that you now have a way to deal with them. You can plan to break the habit without experiencing prolonged withdrawal symptoms or other forms of discomfort. This technique alone should provide you with the confidence you need to break the habit. Before you start, however, there are a few more considerations that will make the transition go more smoothly.

TAKING CONTROL OF YOUR LIFE

Without awareness, our habits run our lives. Real choice comes with awareness. We can decide at any time that things will be different. Then we can truly create the life we want.

Changing any habit requires a period of adjustment, as you reprogram the unconscious mind. A good standard is to plan on spending two weeks breaking the old habit and two weeks creating more productive strategies. During this transitional period you have new choices that will set the pace for what you are going to create in your future.

The key, then to changing a habit is to focus on what you are doing and take back your control. Many people deviate from their goals because they have not fully committed to them. With a strong resolve, EFT, and GTT, success is practically guaranteed.

Here are some suggestions for creating a smooth transition.

1. **Prepare yourself emotionally and mentally.** Write a list of all of the emotions, limiting beliefs, and doubts you have that could prevent you from being successful with your goal, and clear them with EFT. Here are some examples:

   - You may be afraid of failure. This often prevents people from attempting to achieve what they want in life. Fortunately, with EFT, you can eliminate it when it comes up.

- You may believe that breaking a habit has to be difficult or painful. We all hear smokers repeat the cry "I need a cigarette" over and over every day. This belief alone sets them up. It can also be eliminated easily with EFT.

- You may not feel that you have enough willpower. Again, you can probably eliminate your self-doubt with EFT.

2. **Examine the spiritual components.** The search that has led to the addiction is generally based on an unconscious desire to feel complete. As was mentioned previously, an addictive person is actually searching for love and wholeness. He or she just forgot who she is. Use the Holistic Process to identify what is needed for healing at all levels.

- Begin to realize that you are lovable, whole and complete just as you are. This is where work on PR may come in handy. On an unconscious level, many people do not feel that they deserve love. Test yourself for "The Levels of PR" in Figure 5.1 before using the Holistic Process. This will give you some information about what is happening in your unconscious mind.

- As you prepare for change, examine any judgments you have toward yourself and release them with EFT and GTT. Use the Unification Process to connect with your Ideal Habit-Free Self. This is a very powerful way to see what is possible, because you already have that ideal within you. You can also maintain your commitment by continuing to visualize this Ideal Self at least a few times a day while you are in the process of changing the habit. This will help you to maintain your resolve.

3. **Eliminate the external factors that might sabotage your plans.** Any healing must consider the impact of your lifestyle

and relationships. The arena where addictions are played out is relationships. Be prepared for how those in your environment are going to react to the changes you initiate. Here are some examples:

- If there are people in your household, office, or general environment who have the same habit or addiction, you need to consider how they might respond to your desire to change. If possible, find a way to enlist their cooperation, and work out a strategy for dealing effectively with the situations you are likely to encounter.

- If there are specific times of the day when you crave the habit, like smoking or eating at break time at work, or having a drink when you come home at night, plan other things to do at those times.

- Free time is a factor, too. What will you do with your time instead of smoking, having that sixth cup of coffee or whatever. Again, it helps to develop strategies ahead of time.

You may also want to refer to Chapter Nine to help you to understand relationship dynamics.

4. **Write a list of all the benefits of breaking the habit, like being smoke-free.** Writing this list will help you to firm up your resolve, and you can refer to it later if doubt sets in. Some questions to ask yourself:

- How will your life change?
- What will the benefits be?
- How will you feel next month if you decide to stop now?
- How will you feel next month if you do not stop now?

5. **Tips for smokers:** In addition to saving hundreds or even

thousands of dollars on cigarettes by quitting, the American Cancer Society reports that the negative physical effects of smoking begin to reverse themselves within a few years of kicking the habit. After ten years, the non-smoker may even return to a normal life expectancy.

- **Plan to quit all at once.** Tapering off is generally not successful, particularly for smoking, because of the prolonged effort. At any rate, you can plan on a smooth transition requiring less effort with the use of EFT.

- **Plan on allowing a month to transition from the old habit to another way of being.** This should be easy with EFT.

- **Make the decision that from the time you set for quitting, you will use EFT instead of lighting the cigarette or whatever.** You can strengthen your resolve if you visualize it. Close your eyes for a moment and see yourself craving the substance or habit and choosing to use EFT rather than going back to the old behavior. Allow yourself to experience the feeling of success as you continue to maintain your goal in this way.

6. **Develop a relationship with your Ideal Self.** As we mentioned before, it helps to contact your Ideal Smoke-Free Self, your Ideal Body or other Ideal Habit-Free Self at least a few times a day. This Ideal Self is already clear of the habit and can help you to maintain your commitment over time.

7. **Decide that you will use EFT to clear any emotions, beliefs or self-doubt that come up** after you "quit," so that you can be emotionally-free as well as substance- or habit-free well into the future.

8. **Set a date.** Once you have addressed all of these factors, you can set a date. You should be ready to change any time you choose. Delay will create room for doubt, so you may want to start right away. Use the Break Thru Process to help you to visualize your upcoming success.

LONG-TERM PLANNING

To ensure continued success for life, you should prepare a strategy for the future. In each of our lives, things happen unexpectedly. If we are not prepared, we may be vulnerable to our old habits. You will want to have a plan in place to use when this happens. It is kind of like having an escape plan in case of a fire. When the unexpected happens, you can follow your plan.

Imagine yourself in the future, in a few possible stressful situations where you might be tempted to return to the old habit. Decide now what you will do, including the use of EFT, GTT, and other ways to reduce stress. Write down the plan along with your list of benefits of ending your habit. It will be easier to choose EFT and GTT over the substance or behavior if you prepare ahead of time. This strategy will stay with you throughout your life, so you know that you will always be free.

CHAPTER FIFTEEN

Reaching Your Ideal Weight

Do not wish to be anything but what you are,
and try to be that perfectly.

- ST. FRANCIS DE SALES

More than thirty percent of the people in this country are overweight. Another twenty-five percent are concerned about their weight. And most of these people can tell you that diets don't work. Nonetheless, with no other choices available and with friends and family prodding them on, they continue to try dieting and fail. In most cases, they end up feeling inadequate and out of control. At least they can take consolation in the fact that they have a lot of company.

Most diets have some common elements:

- Food intake is reduced, often to the point of starvation.

- The types of food eaten are restricted, which creates cravings.

On the other hand, most diets are missing other elements:

- Teaching lifestyle changes needed for long term success.

- Dealing with the EM&S components of weight problems.

The standard diet is doomed from the beginning. If the body believes it is starving, it will do whatever it can to prevent hunger. It will eat. And when foods are restricted, most people respond by wanting them more. This may be an emotional reaction or a physical reaction to the body's need for nutrients. Like the other issues we have explored, the problem is that diets treat the symptoms and not the cause. They rely on willpower; ordering the conscious mind to overrule the impulses coming from the unconscious mind. With overeating, powerful impulses from the unconscious mind will not stop just because the conscious mind has decided to change. Until the underlying reasons for overeating are revealed, attempts to reduce weight are bound to fail.

Less than one percent of those who approach weight control by treating symptoms maintain their goal weight over an extended period of time. The other ninety-nine percent feel like failures and may even end up heavier than when they started.

WHY DO PEOPLE EAT?

It is fascinating to ask people with weight problems why they eat. There can be a variety of responses, most of which have nothing to do with hunger or maintaining a healthy body. People with weight problems generally say they eat to satisfy emotional needs. Eating may reduce stress, relieve boredom, serve as a reward, fill their need for love, and so on. Until they understand all of the needs, their chances for success are limited. They are likely to find any attempts to lose weight a battle of wills between the part who wants to lose weight and the part or parts who want to have food to fill emotional needs.

MARILYN'S PROCESS ON WEIGHT

In one of our classes, Jane worked with a woman we will call Marilyn who was having trouble losing weight. Marilyn thought she wanted to be thinner, but muscle testing gave a different picture. She tested weak for the statement "I want to be my ideal weight," and the statement "I will become my ideal weight." With the Unification Process, we discovered that an unconscious subpersonality who believed that losing weight made no sense, because when she was thin before, things didn't work out. This part felt frustrated and powerless.

Until she was able to identify this part of herself and change her belief, she could only continue to struggle with her weight. The image she saw of herself was a shapeless figure in a loose dress, with no waist and a bloated face.

Fortunately, EFT came to the rescue. After clearing the powerlessness with EFT, the shapeless figure started shrinking. Marilyn now saw herself in a bathing suit holding her arms up in a "V" for victory. She could even feel her power coming back. She had made contact with her Ideal Body. She then tested strong both for "I want to be my ideal weight," and "I will become my ideal weight."

THE HOLISTIC APROACH TO EATING

As you might suspect, people who are naturally at their ideal weight respond to the question of why they eat quite differently than those with weight problems do. They may even think it is a trick question. They eat because they are hungry.

Fortunately, with EFT and GTT, you can approach weight loss holistically, treating your whole self, and reaching your ideal weight naturally. Unless there are medical restrictions that need to be addressed, most people may even be able to continue eating most of the same foods, if they want to.

We also have a booklet called *The Holistic Approach to Eating* that is described in Appendix B. It deals exclusively with weight issues, and provides a comprehensive approach to successfully reaching your ideal weight and feeling good about yourself. The key to *The Holistic Approach to Eating* is to become more sensitive to the body. It shifts the focus on using food to meet the needs of the mind and emotions to feeding and nurturing the body.

Oddly enough, when we overeat to appease our emotional needs, the body suffers, having to digest quantities and types of food that create physical discomfort and a foggy mind. Marilyn's process was a good example of this: She saw herself as shapeless and bloated. When you uncover the problem with the Unification Process and balance the emotions with EFT, everything changes. In Marilyn's case, she saw her shapeliness return as she reconnected with her Ideal Body. From this new perspective, she should actually want to eat less. She will also want to eat foods that nourish the body rather than appeasing the mind and emotions.

Here is a quote from the booklet:

Diets rely on the conscious mind to control the responses coming from the unconscious. What we don't know is that it's just like trying to swim upstream on a river with a strong current. You might succeed for awhile, but even if you do, you have to keep working just to stay even and eventually simply get tired of the effort, and allow yourself to float downstream, back into the old way. In comparison, using a natural approach, you get the conscious mind and the unconscious mind working together. Then the way to success is like floating on a calm lake with clear water. You know exactly what is happening and how to deal with it.

UNDERSTANDING WHY YOU EAT

Here are some suggestions to get you started toward reaching your ideal weight.

1. Start by muscle testing for "The Levels of PR" described in Figure 5.1. Trying to lose weight when PR is present is generally a fruitless endeavor. People with weight problems usually do not even want to lose weight unconsciously. This makes sense. They have gravitated to their current weight in response to the programming in their unconscious minds.

2. Write a list of reasons why you eat other than hunger. When the list is complete, go through each one and write the emotions you experience when you have cravings for food. Some common reasons why people eat:

   • To reduce stress.

   • To give themselves a treat.

   • To cover up loneliness.

   • To overcome boredom.

   • To ease pain.

3. If you test weak for wanting to reach your ideal weight and do not know why, use the Unification Process to find out more. Before starting, refer to your list of reasons why you eat. Then do the process, focusing on one of the times you crave food. This will expose your unconscious motivations and put you in

touch with your Ideal Body. Focusing on this body at least a few times a day can help you to maintain your resolve. With these techniques, losing weight should be like floating on a calm lake with clear water. If you focus on your Ideal Body and eating lightly, you will naturally gravitate to your ideal weight.

Understanding why you eat corresponds to the first step toward "Taking Control of Your Life," which was a section in the previous chapter. You should refer to this chapter, and follow the steps to take back control as you prepare to head toward your ideal weight.

YOUR COMMITMENT

EFT is an amazing tool that can jump-start any weight loss program, but the commitment has to come from you. You have a choice. This book provides some of the most powerful tools available today. You have to provide the desire to change.

You also need to focus on loving yourself. Dr. Bob Schwartz, PhD, describes the importance of love in his entertaining and enlightening book *Diets Don't Work.*

> When you're gentle with yourself, the positive and creative aspects just bubble to the surface without any effort. The attractive and thin person inside you will come forth when he or she knows that it's safe. A loving, accepting, nurturing environment will draw the thin person out much faster.

With the Unification Process, you will probably find that your Ideal Body also wants to be physically active. Exercise is as important to your overall well-being as eating well. If you want to achieve your Ideal Body, you also have an opportunity to address your need for exercise in the next chapter. The two go hand-in-hand.

CHAPTER SIXTEEN

Increasing Physical Activity and Performance

*You must learn to be still
in the midst of activity and to be
vibrantly alive in repose.*

- INDIRA GANDHI

We all are aware of the benefits of regular physical activity, but most of us lead relatively inactive lives. We know that exercise is fun for children, but people usually lose the enjoyment of movement by the time they become adults. Most American adults are sedentary. With responsibilities for career and family, we simply can't "find the time" to exercise. We tell ourselves that we will start soon, but soon never comes. We continue to find ourselves becoming older and less fit. This phenomenon is not just dangerous for the body; we also suffer emotionally and mentally. Our self-esteem continues to descend, and we miss the fun we had in our youth.

Fortunately, it is never too late to change. In his book *Better Health with Self-Hypnosis*, Frank S. Caprio, MD, says that the key to reversing the aging process is exercise. He maintains that people in their 60's and 70's can rebuild the vitality they had 20 or so years ago and enjoy a more fulfilling life.

Moderate exercise can help you to do all of these things:

- Improve circulation.
- Reduce blood pressure.
- Release nervous tension.
- Tone fatigued muscles.
- Reduce fat.
- Improve stamina.
- Increase energy and self-confidence.
- Improve overall health.

The body has an amazing ability to improve at any age. John Douillard describes this in his book *Body, Mind and Sport*. He reports that studies of people in their nineties have shown that a program of moderate exercise can produce a 300 percent increase in strength in just six to eight weeks. The potential for improvement stays with us throughout our lives.

ACTIVATE YOURSELF WITH EFT AND GTT

The techniques in this book can make exercise as exciting and fun for adults as it is for children. When we think of exercise, many of us imagine ourselves pushing our bodies to exhaustion and hating every minute of it. Through negative programming, we have alienated the body and the mind. The best way to develop an exercise plan is to find activities that are comfortable and stimulating for both the body and the mind. Here are some suggestions:

- Muscle test for "The Levels of PR" in Figure 5.1. Use a phrase like "this inertia" or "this lack of physical activity." If you determine that you do not want to exercise, you can use the Unification Process to find out why and get yourself back on track with your Ideal Physically Active Self.

- Write a list of physical activities you think you would enjoy. You can include more than one type of exercise and will be much more successful if you focus on having fun.

- Clear your fears of failure and humiliation with EFT.

- Connect again with your Ideal Physically Healthy Self and address any concerns this part has about physical activity. As we have suggested with other issues, maintaining contact with this ideal can also help you to maintain your resolve over time.

We also recommend consulting a physician to determine what form and degree of exercise is best for you before starting on any exercise program.

ATHLETIC PERFORMANCE

Even those who participate in regular physical activity can improve their performance and enjoyment with EFT and GTT. Mental focus is an integral part of success in any activity. More and more professional athletes are attributing their amazing feats as much to their mental conditioning as their physical training. In their book *Hypnosis for Change,* Josie Hadley and Carol Staudacher mention a sports psychologist who credits the power of the mind for 80 to 90 percent of an

Olympic athlete's success. Having a clear head, of course, requires releasing emotions like anxiety, fear and doubt that can prevent you from staying focused.

You can use EFT and GTT for improvement in any athletic activity, including tennis, golfing, swimming, weight training, running, walking, bowling skiing, basketball etc. Here are some suggestions:

- **Increase your ability.** Release any anxiety, fear, doubt or other emotions that prevent you from staying focused. You can do this by focusing on how you feel just before you start to play, such as when your are about to serve the ball in a tennis game or drive the ball down the fairway in a golf game. You can probably release any troubling emotions, beliefs, or judgments with EFT. If you want to go deeper, you can use the Unification Process.

- **Improve your concentration.** Use the Unification Process to connect with your Ideal Athlete. Once you have made this connection, you can focus on that part of yourself while you are engaged in the athletic activity.

- **Enjoy yourself more.** Connecting with your Ideal Athlete will also help you to have more fun with whatever activity you choose.

Gary Craig has several reports on his Web site from top athletes who have been impressed with EFT. The first comes from Pat Ahearne, a professional baseball player in the Australian Baseball League, who worked using EFT with a psychologist named Steve.

Steve and I worked together using EFT to lessen or eliminate the mental and emotional barriers preventing my consistently producing my best games as a pitcher. The results were astounding. I had more consistency, better command of my pitches and accomplished it in big games with less mental effort. ...With EFT, I found the mental edge that raises an athlete from average to elite. I used the techniques to capture the MVP and Perth Heat and the Australian Baseball League Pitcher of the Year Awards.

I am so amazed with the effectiveness of EFT that I've made it as important a part of my baseball routine as throwing or running or lifting weights. The title "Emotional Freedom Techniques" certainly does fit.

The second report comes from a golfer named Steve with a six handicap. Steve used EFT to reduce the anxiety he felt before hitting the ball. He was able to consistently reduce his handicap by 33 percent with EFT. You can find more information about both of these athletes at www.emofree.com.

IMPROVING ALL TYPES OF PERFORMANCE

The techniques in this chapter for improving athletic performance apply equally to performance in school, business, public speaking, or any other activity you engage in. With EFT and GTT, you can increase your skills, improve your concentration and enjoy yourself more with everything you do. The next chapter focuses on other ways to achieve genuine freedom in your life.

CHAPTER SEVENTEEN

Achieving Genuine Freedom

The purpose of life, after all, is to live it,
to taste experience to the utmost,
to reach out eagerly and without fear
for newer and richer experience.

- ELEANOR ROOSEVELT

We have explored a variety of ways that you can help yourself and others to create a life filled with joy, love, and freedom, which are the keys to true fulfillment. If you are new to self-exploration, the path to freedom may seem a bit rocky at first. Each of us starts by releasing the power the past holds on us, which shows up in the fears, phobias, addictions, anger and other emotions that can control us throughout our lives. As the forest begins to clear, the path becomes smoother. We can move more freely and begin to glimpse possibilities for ourselves that would have been unimaginable before.

The rate you progress on the path is completely up to you. If you devote just fifteen to thirty minutes each day to EFT and GTT, your life will most likely change for the better. As you begin to free yourself of some of the unpleasant emotions that hold you back, you ban begin to focus more on achieving your dreams and goals. This chapter provides some suggestions to help you along. First you need to understand the difference between achieving what you want and getting what society would like you to want.

Society's Influence

We have seen how society influences us. From the time we are born, we learn to focus our energy and attention on the outside world. We are taught that if we study harder, we will do better in school. Similarly, we believe that if we practice more, we can improve our performance in sports, playing musical instruments, dancing or anything in our lives. And, when we become adults, we believe that if we work harder, we will earn more money and find more happiness.

This is true to a degree, but it is only part of the equation. In addition to focusing on how to create from the outside in, we need to focus on creating from the inside out. Money alone does not bring happiness and fulfillment. The key to having the love, joy, and freedom lies within each one of us. We need to slow down enough in the busy pace of modern life to look within ourselves.

A FINAL LOOK AT PSYCHOLOGICAL REVERSAL

We have discussed how we unconsciously sabotage our goals in different parts of our lives. A conscientious person may spend years trying unsuccessfully to lose weight only to find that her unconscious mind has no desire to lose any weight at all.

People respond differently to the events in their lives. As we mentioned earlier, most of us have PR in one or a small number of areas in our lives, so we are able to succeed easily in some areas and encounter difficulty in other areas. A small percentage of people has very little PR and is able to overcome seemingly insurmountable obstacles with ease. And, on the other end of the scale, there are people for whom any small obstacle seems impossible to overcome or for whom almost everything seems to go wrong.

Switched Circuit

We need to look at our tendencies to sabotage ourselves without judgment, and remember that PR is a polarity problem, not a character defect. People who are reversed in most areas of their lives have what is known by some as Massive Psychological Reversal or a Switched Circuit. Dr. James V. Durlacher describes this phenomenon in his book *Freedom From Fear Forever*.

In people with a Switched Circuit, the energy flow through the body is disturbed in a way that makes both physical and emotional healing difficult. They will test weak for achieving positive results in most aspects of life. They have difficulty improving their health and in reaching their goals. They tend to procrastinate and are prone to self-destructive thinking. This naturally creates a pessimistic attitude, so a Switched Circuit may also be linked to depression. It may even create a reluctance to try to change or seek help. Homeless people and criminals are extreme examples.

There is a way to test for a Switched Circuit that Dr. Stephen Paul Shepard describes in his book on muscle testing, *Healing Energies.* The receiver holds one arm out in the usual way for testing. Then perform the following tests:

1. Hold the receiver's free hand about an inch above the head with the palm facing down toward the top of the head. Now test the strength of the extended arm.

2. Turn the receiver's free hand over and hold it about an inch above the head with the palm facing upward and the back of the hand facing the top of the head. Now test the strength of the extended arm again.

When the energy flow through the body is healthy, the receiver will test strong with the palm facing down and weak with the palm facing up. If he or she tests weak with the palm facing down and strong with the palm facing up, his circuits are switched. Returning to Gary Craig's description of Psychological Reversal, it is like the body's main battery has been installed upside down. You cannot access the power in the battery until you turn it around.

Fortunately, this condition is correctable with EFT. Since it is generally linked with procrastination, we have the individual perform the Short or Complete Sequence of EFT using the affirmation "Even though I have this procrastination, I deeply and completely accept myself," followed by tapping on the normal points using "this procrastination" as the reminder phrase. If you have a Switched Circuit and suffer from a chronic illness or depression, you may want to substitute one of those for procrastination.

We recommend repeating the process every waking hour for a week, then retesting the Switched Circuit. You may need to focus strongly on your goal to do this, because you will probably tend to procrastinate. Remember that it only takes about a minute to complete this procedure. And if you miss it once or twice and feel defeated, just do EFT on the feelings of being defeated, then proceed with your goal.

Even if you test normal for a Switched Circuit, most of us procrastinate. And wherever we procrastinate, we are holding back energy that could be used productively. Looking at what is happening when you procrastinate is a way to uncover emotional blockages, limiting beliefs, and judgments that need to be released. You can do this by focusing on a time when you tend to put things off and using either the Holistic Process or the Unification Process. You may be surprised at your unconscious reasons for procrastinating.

APPRECIATING YOURSELF

Figure 17.1 provides some statements you may want to muscle test. This list is a variation on statements developed by a psychologist named Larry P. Nims, who also uses meridian-based techniques. You will want to test positive for all of these things to move forward into a life filled with joy, love, and freedom.

As a note, if you test negative for "I want to be happy" and positive for "I want to be miserable," chances are that you have a Switched Circuit. When this is the case, you can correct the reversal by doing the short or complete EFT sequence using the affirmation " Even though I am miserable, I deeply and completely accept myself," and the reminder phrase "this misery." To correct it permanently, we recommend repeating the procedure every waking hour for a week, then retesting the Switched Circuit on a regular basis. You may also explore the problem more deeply with GTT. This is even more likely to produce a permanent change.

FIGURE 17.1
MORE STATEMENTS FOR MUSCLE TESTING

- I am a good person.

- I want to be happy.

- I want to be successful.

- I deserve to be loved.

- I deserve good things in life.

- I have many talents and skills.

- I have a resourceful mind.

- I am a capable person.

- I have a good body.

- I want to be healthy.

Switched Circuit and Neurological Disorganization

In his book *Freedom From Fear Forever*, Dr. James V. Durlacher states that you can detect Neurological Disorganization with the Switched Circuit Test. If a person tests strong for both hand positions, he or she has Neurological Disorganization. Use the procedure for correcting Neurological Disorganization described in Chapter Six before going further.

Affirmations

Since a Switched Circuit is related to negative thinking, you may also want to interject some positive thoughts on a regular basis. Connecting with your Ideal Self provides positive input that you can reinforce whenever you think of it. Gary Craig calls the thoughts that constantly run through our heads "the writing on our walls." If you are writing a lot of negative stuff, this is what you will most likely have in your life. If you write more positive things, your life will change for the better. It can help to write down positive thoughts and place them in prominent locations in your home like on the refrigerator door and the bathroom mirror. This will remind you of your goals

LIVING YOUR HEART'S DESIRE

Some years ago, we (Phillip and Jane) reached a point in our lives where all of our basic needs were met. We both had jobs that supported us well. We had two cars and a home in a nice neighborhood. We started to look around and realized that something was still missing. What we were missing was a way to bring a more soulful perspective to our daily activities and goals in life. We wanted to create our heart's desire.

As our awareness of what was happening to us grew, we began to focus more of our attention on what we really wanted. This is the first key. You have to know what you really want. It is similar to creating a map of where you want to go. If you just set out going north, because the freeway is the widest and the signs are largest, you may discover after driving for awhile that it is not taking you where you want to go at all. You turn off and start to go east for awhile, only to find that what you are seeking does not seem to be in that direction either. After a few more turns, you may be completely lost, or find yourself back where you started. Meanwhile, time has passed and you are no closer to reaching your goal than you were when you started.

Setting Your Course

Here are the steps we took to create genuine freedom. When we examined our lives from a soulful perspective, we realized that we wanted to be able to experience more of the varied cultures and natural beauty in the world around us. We wanted our occupations to include travel and helping others. We also wanted to create loving relationships with people with whom we could share our experiences. And we wanted to have enough time and money to make these things possible.

So how would we achieve these things? Many people rely on the lottery to create the freedom they want, but common sense tells us that this is not going to be the solution for most people. We decided to start by incorporating more of the things we wanted on a regular basis. This put us on a course that allowed us to create more and more of our heart's desire over time.

We now see movement on this course as a continuum, which goes from painful emotions and limitation at one end to joy, love and freedom at the other end. Wherever you are on this continuum, each of your choices leads you more in one direction or the other. You may not believe that you could have joy, love, and freedom in all aspects of your life, but if you start taking little steps in that direction, you will gradually build more and more.

CONTINUUM FOR CREATING YOUR HEART'S DESIRE

From	To
Pain and	Joy, Love,
Limitation	and Freedom

There are some helpful questions you can ask yourself if you are not sure what you really want in your life. If you are in a meaningful relationship or marriage, you will probably want to do this with your partner. If you have children or an extended family, you will want to include them as well in whatever way is appropriate for their ages. We suggest that each of you write your own lists, then discuss them together so you can begin to see how you can help each other to achieve your goals. There may be things that you will want to do together and other things that you will each do individually.

Here are the questions:

1. **If there were not limitations of place, time or money, where would you want to be, what would you want to do, and what would you want to have?** For those of you who have spent many years trying to get where you want to go, you may begin to think of all of the fun things you would want to do. We suggest focusing on the heart, which is the seat of your

soul's desire. Then write down in your journal all of the things
your heart desires, and what you would want to have to create
a life filled with joy.

After you have gone through the fun things, you may also
want to focus on your true purpose and the deeper meaning of
life. We all came here for a reason, and most of us have something to share with others, which is our genuine occupation.
You may find that you are already in the right occupation; you
may find that you would rather be doing something else.

2. **If you want to have a lot of money, what does it represent
to you?** We already discussed the relationship between money,
possessions, and fulfillment at the end of Chapter Eight. For
some people, money represents freedom, for others it represents happiness, security, stability, power, a way to achieve
relaxation, or any of a number of other things.

15.   It may not take as much money to have a life filled
with joy, love, and freedom as you would think at first. You
may be able to achieve more security, stability, power, and relaxation immediately by using the processes in this book. It is
not that there is anything wrong with having money. You just
need to understand that if you have blockages, money may not
be the whole solution. You also need to know what is missing
within you and set out to achieve emotional freedom now.
Money may come more easily as a natural result. When you
have finished looking at what money means to you, you may
want to make some adjustments to your list.

3. **If your life ended today, which of the things on your list
would be most meaningful to you?** Maybe this question will
provide new things to add, maybe other items will be less important. You can use this question to prioritize the items on
your list.

Clearing The Forest

When you have established your course, you are ready to set off. You will also want to look at what you are attracting in your life, so that you can clear any trees that are in your way as you move forward. You can make adjustments as your goals change over time. This kind of soul-searching usually raises other questions of a more spiritual nature, which we address in our next book, *Getting Thru to Your Soul*. This book focuses on spiritual growth and manifesting your Soul's purpose.

From the Soul's perspective, what we have in our lives is a reflection of who we are and the lessons we are learning.

In our discussion of weight, we mentioned that each of us gravitates to the weight that is most comfortable to the unconscious mind. In reality, we gravitate to whatever is most comfortable for the unconscious mind in every aspect of life.

The next key is to find out why you have not already manifested your heart's desire in all aspects of your life. You have to look at what is standing in your way. Start identifying the trees in your emotional forest and clear them with out EFT and GTT, so you can move freely wherever you want to go. This book provides all the techniques you need to fulfill your true potential. If you never seem to be able to make ends meet, you need to change that. If you never have time to do the things you enjoy, you need to change that, too. If you are not able to create loving relationships in your life, you will probably want to understand why.

Jane had a big awakening when she reached the age of 40.

There were so many things she had been putting off for that elusive time in the future when everything would be easier, that she was not experiencing much joy. With the completion of another decade, Jane saw clearly that if she did not create those experiences for herself now, she could easily go on that way for the rest of her life. Putting what we really want off is common, but we risk the likely possibility that the time we are waiting for will never come. For this reason, we suggest starting now, regardless of how old you are.

You may also want to consider how the other people in your life will respond to your decision to fulfill your heart's desire. Many people find themselves in non-supportive relationships or have friends or relatives who discourage them from going in their own direction. You may want to review the suggestions on relationships in Chapter Nine and examine how you can create healthy boundaries.

As you travel down the path, you need to monitor your progress. Life continues to bring challenges. We look at how we are doing almost every day and keep clearing any limitations we discover. In this way, all of the events of our lives take on a deeper meaning, and we continue to expand and grow.

THE KEYS TO YOUR SUCCESS

Remember that the keys to your success are in your hands. In the Healing High-Rise there are many doors to open. The techniques you will find in each room hold hidden treasures. You can unlock possibilities you might not have imagined before. What you will discover can be quite profound, opening you to a whole new level of awareness, leading to a life filled with joy, love, freedom and genuine fulfillment.

Alternatives

The use of meridian-based techniques is just in its infancy. As more people experiment with the possibilities, new discoveries are being made, providing a wide range of approaches to explore. This section focuses on some alternatives we have encountered.

TOUCH AND BREATHE (TAB)

A psychologist named John H. Diepold, Jr. has developed an alternative to the tapping used in the EFT sequences. Instead of tapping on each of the points, he simply touches each point lightly with the fingertip while taking one full inhale and one full exhale. He has found his success with this approach to be comparable to EFT.

TAB is an option some people may find more gentle and less attention-calling for use in public situations. Dr. Diepold believes that it may be particularly effective for people with physical conditions that preclude the use of tapping and for people who may find the tapping frightening.

You can find an article by Dr. Diepold with detailed information about TAB on Gary Craig's Web site, which is listed in Appendix C.

BACH FLOWER REMEDIES

In his book *Freedom From Fear Forever*, Dr. James Durlacher presents a group of meridian-based techniques based on the work of Roger Callahan. Among other things, he recommends using Bach Flower Remedies to help overcome phobias and limiting beliefs. A homeopathic physician named Dr. Edward Bach developed these remedies during the early 1900's. They are composed of flower essences in a water base. Altogether, there are 38 different remedies, each of which is reported to relieve specific emotional symptoms.

In particular, Dr. Durlacher recommends using Bach Rescue Remedy, which is a combination of five of the flower essences. He feels that Rescue Remedy helps to facilitate recovery from Massive Psychological Reversal, which we describe in Chapter Seventeen. You may also experience a temporary case of Massive PR during times of extreme duress, like following a traumatic event, an accident, or a similar situation. We find that Rescue Remedy helps in returning to a state of balance.

USING A SURROGATE WITH EFT

There may be times when it is not possible to perform EFT or muscle testing on the person who is experiencing difficulty.

You may also want to use EFT to help a baby or an animal. In such cases, using a surrogate is an option.

This approach may be a bit far out for some. To others is may seem quite natural, as it does to us. Our experience with Reiki, long-distance healing, and clairvoyant techniques includes receiving and sending energy long distance. In any case, when you have no other option, you might want to give it a try.

To serve as a surrogate, you perform the EFT sequences on yourself, with the intent of helping another person or being. Similarly, you can perform muscle testing on yourself with the intent to obtain information about another person.

We have had success using surrogate EFT with our dog who has asthma attacks. When an attack comes on, Jane usually sits with him on the couch and places one hand on his shoulder to create a connection. He seems to understand what is occurring and holds still. Then she goes through the affirmation and the Short Sequence, while focusing on helping him with his asthma. He generally stops wheezing within one or two rounds of the Short Sequence and looks completely relaxed. She has had similar results with hiccups and sneezing attacks.

Jane likes having the physical connection, but if this is not possible, it is not necessary to touch the individual you are working with to achieve results. As those who use Reiki and other energetic healing techniques understand, it does not matter where the other individual is located.

With distance healing, you are working with your intent, moving beyond the barriers of time and space. The key is to hold your focus on what you are doing.

On Gary Craig's Web site, there are some examples of people who report using surrogate EFT successfully. Refer to Appendix C. Now we will explore another use for your intent.

CREATING HARMONY

The subjects of surrogate testing and the power of our intent are fascinating. They may be difficult for some people to grasp without tangible proof. Fortunately, you can easily demonstrate the power of intent with muscle testing.

In Chapter Five, we discussed using muscle testing with white sugar as a way to show how the foods you ingest affect your body. As mentioned there, most people have a weak response when they hold white sugar over their stomachs and muscle test. This weak response indicates that the sugar is weakening to the body. If you have not done so already, we suggest trying this test. If you find that you test weak for white sugar, you have the opportunity to demonstrate the power of your intent. If you do not test weak for white sugar, you can test some other foods until you find one that produces a weak response.

When you have found a food that produces a weak muscle test response, you are ready to test the power of your intent. Before you start, confirm that you are in a centered state. Then hold the food in your hand and focus your intent on bringing it into harmony with your energetic frequency. Imagine that its energetic structure is changing to come into harmony with your own. After about a minute, it should feel like it is done.

The final step is to test the food again with Kinesiology, using the same method as the original test. In our experience, the harmonized food will usually test strong. The purpose of the test is to show the power of intent and the benefits of simply asking the substances that you ingest, use on your body, and have in your environment to come into harmony with you. This is basically the same idea as praying before eating a meal and asking for your food to be blessed.

You can do a similar test with a computer. Many people test weak when they sit in front of a computer and focus on how it is affecting them energetically. If you get a weak response, focus your intent for a moment on bringing the frequency emitted by the computer into harmony with your energetic frequency and retest. You will probably test strong.

In this appendix, we have explored variations on the use of EFT. In Appendix B, you will find resources that include EFT and other meridian-based techniques, along with some recommended reading.

Resources

AUDIO TAPES AND VIDEO TAPES

Getting Thru to Your Emotions with EFT: Video Tapes.
These two tapes present the processes described in this book through real examples and demonstrations. Seeing the techniques in action will help with your timing, precision, and presentation. The videotapes offer different examples of common problems from those covered in the book. The procedures have commentaries by Phillip and Jane Mountrose.

- **Tape One** presents the EFT processes.

- **Tape Two** presents the GTT processes.

Getting Thru to Your Emotions with EFT : Two Audio Tapes.
This two-tape set provides guided versions of the GTT processes presented in this book, with background music. These

tapes allow you to sit or lie back and relax, while we guide you through each of the processes.

Getting Thru to Kids: Problem-Solving with Children Ages 6 to 18: **Two Audio Tapes.** This audio set gives you the essence of Phillip Mountrose's award-winning book, read by the author. Uplifting and easy to follow, great for deepening your communication skills.

Centering and Reaching for the Light: **One Audio Tape.** This lucid tape explores the power and importance of becoming centered in your True Self, your Soul, and the journey toward embodying it in your daily life. Includes a powerful meditation that you can use regularly. Narrated by Jane Mountrose.

BOOKS FROM HOLISTIC COMMUNICATIONS

The Holistic Approach to Eating: Lose Extra Weight and Keep It Off for Life by Jane Mountrose
This 82-page booklet gives you the keys to losing and maintaining your weight for life. Learn the reasons traditional diets fail and techniques that really work. Make real progress and feel good about yourself.

Getting Thru to Kids: Problem Solving with Children Ages 6 to 18 by Phillip Mountrose
Learn five steps to problem-solving with children, improving trust, honesty, school attitude, and friendships. Jack Canfield, co-author of *Chicken Soup for the Soul* series, says, "This book offers a simple and effective method to create peace and harmony in the home and high self-esteem in your children."

Tips and Tools for Getting Thru Kids: Innovative Approaches for Pre-schoolers to Teens by **Phillip Mountrose**
25 dynamic suggestions that teach parents and educators about themselves as well as their children. "An accomplishment well worth studying," says Michael Gurian, author of *A Fine Young Man* and *The Wonder of Boys.*

Ordering information for the above materials is located at the end of this book.

RECOMMENDED BOOKS

Chopra, Deepak, *Quantum Healing.* New York: Bantam, 1990. Exploring the frontiers of mind/body medicine.

Diamond, John. *Life Energy.* New York: Paragon House, 1990. Ways to use muscle testing and the meridians to unlock the hidden power of your emotions.

Douillard, John. *Body, Mind and Sport.* New York: Crown Publishing: 1995. The mind-body guide to lifelong fitness and being your personal best.

Durlacher, James. *Freedom From Fear Forever.* Tempe, Arizona: Van Ness Publishing, 1995. This book describes the meridian-based techniques developed by Dr. Durlacher, based on the discoveries of Roger Callahan.

Hadley, Josie and Staudacher, Carol. *Hypnosis for Change.* Oakland, California: New Harbinger, 1995. A practical manual of proven hypnotic techniques.

Jampolsky, Lee. *Healing the Addictive Mind*. Berkeley, California: Celestial Arts Publishing, 1991. A guide to freeing yourself from addictive patterns and relationships.

Kenyon, Tom. *Brain States*. Naples, Florida: United States Publishing, 1994. A book that explores the limitless potentials of the human mind.

Schwartz, Bob. *Diets Don't Work*. Houston Texas: Breakthru Publishing, 1992. A practical guide on how to lose weight and keep it off forever.

Shepard, Stephen Paul. *Healing Energies*. Provo, Utah: Woodland Health Books, 1983. A system of preventing disease by muscle testing and studying the blueprint of the body.

Siegel, Bernie. *Peace, Love and Healing*. New York: Harper & Row, 1989. An exploration of bodymind communication and the path to self-healing.

WEB SITES

EFT Sites

The Getting Thru Web Site: This is our site, which has information on EFT and the other books in the Getting Thru series. You will also find information on other healing techniques, spiritual growth, audio tapes, video tapes, personal consultations, seminars, and two free monthly newsletters. URL: http://www.gettingthru.org

Emotional Freedom Techniques: Gary Craig, the originator of EFT, has developed this site. Here you will find extensive information and support for EFT users. You can also sign up for Gary's e-mail forum and receive regular updates on case histories and recommended uses of EFT.
URL: http://www.emofree.com

Association for Meridian Therapies UK: Promoting EFT and similar techniques in the UK and other EU countries.
URL: http://www.meridiantherapies.co.uk

Sites on Other Meridan-Based Therapies

Be Set Free Fast Method (BSFF): Dr. Larry Nim's site, devoted to behavioral and emotional symptom elimination training for resolving excess emotion: fear, anger, sadness and trauma.
URL: http://members.aol.com/eliums/bsff.html

Energy Psychology and Psychotherapy: A collection of approaches to psychological treatment developed by Dr. Fred Gallo, which address bioenergy systems in the diagnosis and treatment of psychological problems.
URL: http://www.energysych.com

Tapas Acupressure Technique (TAT): A meridian-based technique, developed by Tapas Fleming, which has shown extraordinary promise in the treatment of traumatic stress, allergic reactions, and negative emotions.
URL: http://www.tat-intl.com

Thought Field Therapy (TFT): A site devoted to the techniques of Dr. Roger Callahan, the psychologist who made the first discoveries that lead to the development of EFT and other meridian-based therapies.

URL: http://www.tftrx.com

Glossary

Acupuncture Point: A term derived from traditional Chinese medicine referring to points on the body located along the energy meridians. Stimulating these points balances the flow of energy through the meridians and restores normal function to various parts of the body, along with balancing the emotions.

Acute Condition: A condition that begins quickly and is intense or sharp, then slows after a short time; it can be sharp or severe. When used in reference to a physical condition, it generally pertains to a recent disturbance or injury.

Apex Problem: An EFT term referring to a form of denial that some people experience in relation to subtle energy techniques. Their limited belief systems do not include the possibility that these techniques could produce rapid and profound changes. When the changes occur, these people block out their memories of the former problems.

Aspect: An EFT term referring to a specific part of a problem. An emotional pattern may have one or more aspects.

Chronic Condition: A disease or disorder that develops slowly and persists for a long period of time. It can sometimes remain for the person's lifetime. Chronic conditions often relate to core patterns of emotions, beliefs and judgments, and deep aspects of the Self.

EFT: Emotional Freedom Techniques. A series of meridian-based healing processes developed by Gary Craig and Adrienne Fowlie, based on the discoveries of Dr. Roger Callahan.

EM&S: Emotional, Mental, and Spiritual.

Energy Toxins: An EFT term referring to energies and substances that irritate the energy system. Energy toxins include substances that are ingested or in contact with the body, along with negative energies in the environment.

Gamut Point: A point located on the back of the hand, which is also known as the brain balancing point. It is used for the Nine Gamut Process and the Floor-to-Ceiling Eye Roll.

Generalization Effect: An EFT term that describes how clearing achieved with one aspect of an emotional pattern generalizes over the entire emotional pattern after neutralizing some of the aspects.

Getting Thru Techniques: A group of processes that are designed to help individuals to bring greater awareness to what is happening in their unconscious minds, to clear any blockages they encounter, and to integrate the changes into their conscious awareness. These processes help individuals to progress in their personal and spiritual growth, with the ultimate goal of achieving joy, love, and freedom in all aspects of life.

GTT: Getting Thru Techniques.

Holistic: Related to or concerned with integrated whole or complete systems rather than with analyzing or treating separate parts. In relation to healing, this term commonly refers to dealing with the body, emotions, mind, and spirit as parts of an integrated whole.

Holistic Hypnotherapy: A state-of-the-art approach to hypnotherapy that includes the body, emotions, mind, and spirit. It provides ways to tap into the vast resources each person has in the unconscious mind that can lead to an expanded sense of fulfillment and wholeness.

Ideal Self: A GTT term referring to an integrated part of the True Self or Soul. Each person has an Ideal Self related to each aspect of life. Some examples are the Ideal Body, the Ideal Healthy Self, the Ideal Stress-Free Self, and the Ideal Physically Active Self. These ideal selves already know how to create health, joy, love, and freedom in our lives.

Intermittent: When used in reference to a physical disorder, pertains to a condition that alternates between periods of activity and inactivity. This may include symptoms like headaches, asthma attacks, and other disorders that come and go.

Kinesiology: The use of muscle testing to access information from the unconscious mind and the body's innate intelligence. It works by testing how the strength of a muscle is affected by focusing on an external stimulus or a part of the body. Kinesiology may be used to test how the body is affected by different substances, environmental factors, and verbal statements.

Levels of Psychological Reversal (PR): An EFT term referring to specific forms of PR, involving judgments and limiting beliefs that need to be released to achieve success with the EFT tapping sequences.

Massive Psychological Reversal: People who are reversed in most areas of their life have what is known as Massive Psychological Reversal or a Switched Circuit. With these people, the energy flow through the body is disturbed in a way that makes both physical and emotional healing difficult.

Meridian System: A term derived from traditional Chinese medicine referring to a continuous series of energy channels running throughout the body. Each meridian is associated with a particular emotion and organ system. Life force energy, sometimes called "chi," flows through the meridians.

Muscle Testing: The practical use of Kinesiology. By isolating a specific muscle, you can test its response to access conscious and unconscious information.

Neurolinguistic Programming (NLP): A group of techniques and skills that some call the art and science of excellence. NLP includes communication skills that can help anyone to understand how different people experience life, thereby improving both personal and professional relationships. It also includes techniques that are similar to hypnotherapy, which can help with overcoming difficulties and with achieving excellence in all aspects of one's life.

Neurological Disorganization: An EFT term derived from the field of Kinesiology referring to a form of energy blockage that thwarts the effectiveness of the tapping sequences. Neurological Disorganization must be addressed to achieve success with the tapping sequences.

NLP: Neurolinguistic Programming

PEM&S: Physical, emotional, mental, and spiritual; pertaining to the four levels of holistic healing.

PR: Psychological Reversal.

Psychological Reversal (PR): An EFT term referring to the presence of unconscious beliefs and judgments that may prevent an individual from achieving positive results with the EFT tapping sequences. In such cases, the PR must be addressed directly for the tapping sequences to be effective.

Reiki: A hands-on healing approach that involves the transmission of life force energy to specific areas of the body and the surrounding energy field. Reiki includes techniques to use for the physical, emotional, mental, and spiritual levels of healing, along with long distance healing.

Stress: A response to an overwhelming stimulus that activates the body's fight or flight mechanism.

Subpersonality: A part of an individual that has been separated from the wholeness of the soul through difficult or traumatic experiences; sometimes referred to simply as a "part."

SUD Level: A psychology term that stands for "subjective unit of distress." The SUD level measure the intensity of a problem. With EFT, this intensity of emotions and other symptoms is measured on a scale of one to ten, where one is the least intense and ten is the most intense.

Surrogate Muscle Testing: The use of Kinesiology to test responses in another individual. This method is commonly used when an individual is not in a suitable condition to test directly and for testing an individual long distance.

Switched Circuit: Refer to "Massive Psychological Reversal."

Tension Myositis Syndrome (TMS): A term coined by Dr. John Sarno to describe a group of emotionally-induced syndromes that cause pain in the muscles of the neck, back, shoulders, and buttocks.

TFT: Thought Field Therapy.

Thought Field Therapy (TFT): A group of meridian-based processes developed by Dr. Roger Callahan. These techniques form the basis of the Emotional Freedom Techniques, which are the subject of this book.

TMS: Tension Myositis Syndrome.

Index

About the Authors

Phillip and Jane Mountrose have studied and developed self-help, personal growth, and spiritual growth techniques for over twenty-five years. Together they operate the Awakenings Institute For Holistic Studies, a non-profit organization located in California.

PHILLIP MOUNTROSE is a Special Education Teacher, Holistic Hypnotherapist, Reiki Master, NLP Practitioner, and a Minister of Holistic Healing, with over twenty years of classroom experience. He now teaches self-healing and personal growth classes, and works with people individually to help them achieve their goals. He helps people to identify and release their blockages, so they can experience more joy, love and freedom in their lives. He also draws on his extensive teaching experience to help children and families.

Phillip has written two books for communicating with children, entitled *Getting Thru To Kids* and *Tips and Tools for Getting Thru to Kids*. He has a master's in Education from the University of Massachusetts and a master's in Fine Arts from UCLA. Through his media interviews, classes, and consultations, he continues to provide innovative ways to help people improve communication and fulfill their potential.

JANE MOUNTROSE is a Holistic Hypnotherapist, a Reiki Master and a Minister of Holistic Healing with over twenty years of experience as an architect and artist.

In recent years, Jane has focused her attention on helping people to achieve their full potential. Her classes in personal and spiritual growth provide easy-to-use tools derived from Holistic Hypnotherapy, NLP, Reiki, Kinesiology, and clairvoyant reading skills. Jane also maintains a private practice to assist people individually with their growth process.

Jane's consultations include the use of EFT, clairvoyant reading, hypnotherapy, kinesiology, and energetic healing. This unique combination of techniques helps her clients to understand what is holding them back from reaching their full potential and to clear the blockages that are in their way.

Classes and Consultations

Phillip and Jane Mountrose offer personal consultations and teach classes and seminars in EFT, Hypnotherapy, Reiki, Kinesiology, and personal and spiritual growth. For more information about scheduling personal consultations, speaking engagements, and seminars contact:

Phillip and Jane Mountrose
P.O. Box 41152, Sacramento, CA 95841-0152
E-mail: eft@gettingthru.org
Phone Messages: (800) 644-5437

Phillip and Jane welcome your communication, especially your experiences, insights, challenges, and successes with the interactive tools in this book.

For more information, you can also visit their Web site at www.gettingthru.org.

Order Form

ITEM	QUANTITY	COST
Getting Thru to Your Emotions: Book $13.95	_____	_____
Getting Thru to Your Emotions: Two Audio Tapes $16.95	_____	_____
Getting Thru to Your Emotions Videos: Part 1: The EFT Techniques: Video $24.95	_____	_____
Part 2: The GTT Techniques: Video $24.95	_____	_____
Part 1 and Part 2 Videos together $39.95	_____	_____
Holistic Approach to Eating: Booklet $10	_____	_____
Centering and Reaching the Light: Audio $10	_____	_____
Tips and Tools for Getting Thru to Kids: Book $ 12.95	_____	_____
Getting Thru to Kids: Problem-Solving With Children Ages 6-18: Book $11.95	_____	_____
Getting Thru to Kids: 2-tape Audio $16.95	_____	_____
Subtotal		_____

US Shipping $3.00 first item, $.50 each additional item   _____

California residents please add 7.75% for sales tax   _____

AMOUNT ENCLOSED _____

Order Form continued on the next page

<u>Free</u> Email Newsletters (check selections):

Getting Thru to Your Soul ___   Getting Thru to Those You Love ___

E-mail address: _____

Ship to:

Name: _____

Company: _____

Address: _____

City:_____State: _____

Zip: _____Phone:(_____)_____

Payment:

___ Check   ___ Money Order

Credit Card: ___ Visa   ___ Mastercard   ___ Discover

Card Number: _____

Name on Card: _____

Expiration Date: _____/_____

Mail To: Holistic Communications
P.O. Box 41152,
Sacramento, CA 95841-0152

Toll-Free 24 Hour Order Line: (800) 929-7889

For more information, visit our Web site: www.gettingthru.org

Money Back Guarantee!